Making Cards

with Rubber Stamps, Ribbons & Buttons

TweetyJill
PUBLICATIONS
makes you creative!

Published and created by TweetyJill Publications, Inc., 5824 Bee Ridge Road, PMB 412, Sarasota, FL 34233

For wholesale information, please contact Customer Service at www.tweetyjill.com or call 800-595-5497

Printed in China

ISBN 1-891898-08-6

Book Layout: Jill Haglund • Book Design: Laurie Doherty • Editor: Lisa Codianne Fowler • Photography: Herb Booth Studio

Making Cards
with Rubber Stamps, Ribbons & Buttons

Table of Contents

These cards are fun to make! They are colorful, clean and simple, but most of all, EASY! The majority of samples use just one or two playful images per card. Remember, you don't need to have the exact same stamp to make the design work; you can substitute with rubber stamps you already own. But, keep your eye out for new, whimsical images at your local craft and stamp stores, especially those that represent your favorite themes. It's always exciting to add to your collection.

Here are the secrets to most of the cards shown in this book:

1. Start with colorful papers or small ready-made cards with envelopes.
2. Use simple or playful rubber stamp images stamped in colored inks such as pink or turquoise.
3. Attach vibrant ribbons in various patterns by using colorful brads or staples; or just glue the ribbons wherever you want them. Don't be intimidated by the plethora of yummy ribbon designs; mix and match them any way you like.
4. Wrap, tie, twist and "poof" tulle to your heart's content. This gives your cards an interesting texture and a special flair.
5. Add dimension with buttons. Use Glue Dots to adhere single, multi-shaped or stacked buttons to the front and inside of the cards.

These special touches add uniqueness to every card and whimsy to your creations. You'll soon find these greetings are even more fun to give than to make, as these gifts from your heart will be treasured time and again.

Jill Haglund
Founder and President
Tweety Jill Publications

Gussie up,
we're havin' a party

New Year's Eve

Dawne Renee Pitts

materials

Rubber Stamps: Bubbly Border by Stampendous

Pigment Inkpads: ColorBox Pigment Brush (Gold) by Clearsnap

Dye Inkpads: Memories (Black) by Stewart Superior

Papers: Teal Cardstock by Bazzill Basics; White and Black Cardstock: Local Craft Store; Stitched Gallery Floral Paper by Chatterbox

Chipboard Letters: Li'l Davis Designs

Computer Font: Ronita (downloaded from www.fonts.com)

Watercolor Pencils: Local Craft Store

Paint: Crystal Craft Twinkles by Decoart

Metal Items: Rhinestone Brads by SEI

Ribbons: Offray: Local Craft Store

Fabrics: Tulle: Local Craft or Fabric Store

Adhesives: Art Accentz Terrifically Tacky Tape

tip! Be brave! Colorful tulle is available at local craft and fabric stores and is great material to have on hand for cards. If you have never tried it, give it a whirl!

instructions

1. Cover the chipboard letters with the patterned paper; trim out with an Xacto knife and sand the edges. Paint with Twinkle paint.

2. Cut an 8" x 8" square of black cardstock.

3. Cut a 7" x 7" square of the teal cardstock and layer to the black square, using adhesive only on the bottom and sides. Leave the middle and top unattached – the invitation will slip into the square.

4. Attach the top two corners of the teal square with the two gold rhinestone brads.

5. Print your invitation information along the left-hand side on white cardstock; cut the invitation into a tag shape as shown.

6. Add the Bubbly Border stamp to the right side of the information.

7. Using watercolor pencils, color in the champagne bubbles. Instead of using water to blend the colors, take a small amount of the Twinkle paint and dab onto the bubbles – it will gently smear the watercolor pencil a bit and add sparkle.

8. Edge the invitation tag with gold ink.

9. Once the ink and paint have dried, mount the invitation onto a piece of the teal cardstock and trim.

10. Punch a hole in the top of the invitation and run black and gold tulle through it; tie together with a piece of narrow polka-dotted black and white ribbon.

11. Attach the NYE chipboard letters to the front of the card near the top to leave room for ribbon and tulle on bottom.

12. Wrap a piece of wide black and white polka-dotted ribbon around the bottom of the card and begin a knot in the middle of the card. Before you finish the knot, run lengths of black and gold tulle through it and tie those in knots. Once you get the tulle to the desired "poofiness," begin fluffing and snipping the ends to make a very full tulle flower. Tighten the black and white ribbon and trim the ends so they peek out from the bottom of the tulle flower.

Chapter 1
Bring in the
New Year!

Whether it's an invitation to a New Year's Eve Party or best wishes for the year ahead, these cards will put anyone in the party spirit. You'll find plenty of festive images to get started, such as party hats, balloons, blowers, numbers, letters and sentiments. Just add ribbons and tulle, and your cards alone will be cause to celebrate!

Happy New Year!

Amy Wellenstein

materials

Rubber Stamps: Happy New Year; Polka Dot Swirl and Spatter by Stampotique Originals; Party Horn by Whipper Snapper Designs

Pigment Inkpads: VersaFine (Onyx Black) by Tsukineko

Dye Inkpads: Vivid (Spring Green) by Clearsnap; Impress (Pansy) by Tsukineko

Papers: Pink, Black and White Cardstock: Local Craft Store; Purple Clock and Green Scroll by Art Warehouse by Danielle Johnson for Creative Imaginations

Paints: Watercolors: Local Craft Store

Tags: Holiday Metal Rimmed Tags by K&Company

Ribbons: Local Craft Store

Adhesives: Glue Stick; Pop Up Glue Dots and Glue Lines by Glue Dots International; Double-Stick Tape

Tools: Paper Cutter; Sewing Machine

tip! To "mask", stamp image a second time and cut out. Use cutout to cover original stamped design. Next, overstamp with any image you desire, such as a background. Presto! A brand new design.

instructions

1. Stitch small pieces of ribbon to a strip of cardstock to make a decorative border.

2. Tear the edge on a panel of green patterned paper and use glue stick to adhere it to a panel of purple patterned paper.

3. Stamp the layered panel with Polka Dot Swirl using Pansy and Spring Green inks.

4. Adhere the decorative ribbon border to the layered panel.

5. Cover the stitching line on the ribbon border by adhering a strip of ribbon down the center (hiding the ends on the back side of the layered panel).

6. Mount the layered panel to a folded black card.

7. Stamp "Party Horn" on a piece of white cardstock using Onyx Black ink. Color with watercolors.

8. Mask the horn and over-stamp with "Spatter" using Spring Green ink. Layer on black and pink cardstock then adhere to the card using Glue Lines.

9. Tie a pink ribbon through a metal rimmed tag and adhere it to the front of the card using a Pop Up Glue Dot.

You Make My Heart Happy

Dawne Renee Pitts

materials

Rubber Stamps: Emma Stamp by Rubbermoon Stamp Company; Heart Stamp by Kristen Powers for Stampotique Originals; Mara-Mi Alphabet Set by Hampton Art

Pigment Inkpads: ColorBox (Heliotrope) Cat's Eye by Clearsnap

Hybrid Inkpads: Palette Hybrid (Claret) by Stewart Superior

Papers: Birthday Stripe Paper by Tim Coffey for K&Company; Green, Orange, Yellow, Lavender and Blue Cardstock: Local Craft Store

Rub-On Letters: All Mixed Up Expressions in Lilac (Small) by Doodlebug Design

Ribbons: Various Ribbons and Pom Poms by May Arts, Beaux Regards and others: Local Craft Store

Adhesives: Art Accentz Terrifically Tacky Tape by Provo Craft; Glue Dots by Glue Dots International

Tools: Paper Cutter; Paper Edgers (Scallop) by Fiskars; Pinking Shears by Mundial; Bone Folder (A common tool available at local craft stores used to burnish the edge of papers, such as a folded card, to make it lay smooth and flat.)

instructions

1. Cut and fold green cardstock into card. Burnish edge with bone folder. Leave the edges slightly longer; pink the right-hand edges.

2. Cut a piece of K&Company paper and adhere it to the front of the card with tape.

3. Stamp the Rubbermoon image using the Heliotrope ink on yellow cardstock; cut out image with scallop scissors.

4. Use the Doodlebug rub-ons to spell out "whee!"

5. Mount the yellow square onto orange cardstock.

6. Use small scraps of ribbon and tuck under the right edge of the orange square and adhere with glue dots; vary the ends, pinking some and angling others for whimsy and fun. Adhere this piece to blue cardstock.

7. Attach strip of pom poms to front using Glue Dots.

8. Cut out and layer lavender and yellow cardstock for inside of card.

9. Stamp heart stamp with Claret ink and use Doodlebug rub-ons for sentiment.

10. Adhere ribbons to sentiment box; pink and angle randomly.

11. Adhere all to inside of card.

tip! A bone folder comes in handy to give your card a finished look. Burnishing the edge allows for a smooth crease that doesn't crack or break the paper when bent to fold.

Chapter 2 · Friends

    Cards for friends are really extra special because we don't necessarily make them for a specific occasion, such as a birthday, graduation or anniversary. We create them for someone that is meaningful to us. Meaningful enough to sit down and take the time to create a little "something" for them. When I receive a handmade card from a friend, I pin it on the corkboard in my studio to remind me of them, as well as the time they invested in me.

    I agree with the quote, "Time is the most important thing you can give someone." So we've found a way to give time back to you... time to create more than you thought possible. These cards are quick, easy and fun to make, and cheerful enough to inspire anyone! Enjoy your art time and making cards for yourself and others. You deserve it!

Button, Button

Dawne Renee Pitts

materials

Rubber Stamps: Button Cube Stamp by Stampotique Originals; Buttons Lower Case Alphabet Set by PSX

Pigment Inkpads: ColorBox (Heliotrope and Cyan) Cat's Eye by Clearsnap

Dye Inkpads: Memories (Black) by Stewart Superior

Papers: Textured Card-stock by Bazzill Basics; Turquoise Cardstock: Local Craft Store

Metal Items: Eyelets by Doodlebug Design

Ribbons: Black and White Gingham: Local Craft or Fabric Store

Adhesives: Glue Stick

Tools: Paper Cutter; Pinking Shears by Mundial

tip! If you have a friend who collects similar items as you, this is a fun way to share some of your goodies with them!

instructions

1. Cut a piece of Bazzill cardstock and make a matchbook-style card (see photo).

2. Cut a piece of turquoise cardstock and pink one end with pinking shears; adhere to front of card.

3. Stamp buttons using both Heliotrope and Cyan inks. Cut out the stamped images and adhere to card as shown.

4. Set eyelets in two of the buttons as shown and thread with black and white gingham.

5. Stamp "button button" using the PSX button lowercase stamps and use circle punch to punch out letters. Adhere to card as shown.

6. Make a tag out of turquoise cardstock and attach the button card to the tag using the colored brad. Pink the top edge of the tag and tuck tag into matchbook card.

7. Line the bottom of the front of the card with black and white gingham.

8. Handwrite your sentiment on front and inside of card.

Best Buddies

Dawne Renee Pitts

materials

Rubber Stamps: Let's Talk by Rubbermoon Stamp Company; Large Heart by Claudia Rose; Double Heart Stamp by Paper Inspirations; Small Heart Stamp by Hero Arts; Small Star Stamp by Our Lady of Rubber; Antique Alphabet Stamps by PSX; Providence Alphabet Stamps by Making Memories

Pigment Inkpads: Antiquities (Chinese Red) by Ranger Industries

Dye Inkpads: Nick Bantok Van Dyke (Brown and Charcoal Grey) by Ranger Industries; Fresco Chalk Finish Dye Ink (Sicilian Spice, Blue Grotto, Olive Grove and Vatican Wine) by Stampa Rosa

Papers: Malibu Stripe Paper by Sue Dreamer; all others by FoofaLa

Tags: FoofaLa

Metal Items: Pink Snap by Making Memories; Silver Tassie by FoofaLa

Ribbons: Gingham, Ribbons and Rick Rack: Local Craft and Fabric Store

Adhesives: Art Accentz Terrifically Tacky Tape by Provo Craft

Other: Vintage Buttons and Silk Flower

Tools: Paper Cutter; Aging Sponge by FoofaLa; Pinking Shears by Fiskars

instructions

1. Age the mini file folder with Nick Bantok Van Dyke Brown ink using the FoofaLa aging sponge.

2. Cut out a piece of the Malibu Stripe paper and pink the top edge. Attach to front of file folder at an angle.

3. Stamp the "Let's Talk" stamp on the oval tag using the Sicilian Spice ink. Also stamp some stars using the small star stamp. Age the edges of the oval with the Van Dyke Brown ink. Attach across the striped paper at the opposite angle.

4. Cut out initials from the FoofaBets and age the edges with the Van Dyke Brown ink. Attach to the bottom of the oval tag.

5. Stamp "buddy" on the file folder label holder using the Making Memories stamps and Nick Bantok Charcoal Grey ink. Also stamp small stars using the Chinese Red ink.

6. Cut a piece of purple velvet and attach along the bottom of the front of the file folder. Attach a vintage button to one end.

7. Cut out a long piece of the rick rack. Poke two holes in the file folder along the crease and run the rick rack through the holes. Attach a piece of gingham to the top using the FoofaLa tassie.

8. Using the Chinese Red ink, stamp the large heart on the inside cover of the file folder. Attach a FoofaLa definition across the heart.

9. For inside of card, stamp pink tag with Double Heart using Blue Grotto dye ink; adhere button to tag. Add a small tag to the blue harlequin tag with a pink snap; tape to card.

10. Pink polka-dotted FoofaLa paper and stamp "In a friend your find your second self." using Charcoal Grey and Wine dye inks. Tape to inside.

11. Cut out "BBF" from the FoofaBets and age with Van Dyke Brown ink. Layer to the top with tape.

tip! Mini file folders from office supply and craft stores make a snappy card presentation.

materials

Rubber Stamps: Flower Girl Stamp by Stampotique Originals; Faux Post Cube by Just for Fun; Mickey ABC Stamps by EK Success; Mini Mara-Mi Alphabet Set by Hampton Art

Dye Inkpads: Memories (Black) by Stewart Superior

Hybrid Inkpads: Palette Hybrid (Claret) by Stewart Superior

Solvent Ink: StazOn (Jet Black) by Tsukineko

Papers: Mango Tag with Pocket Card by Making Memories; Lime Green Cardstock: Local Craft Store

Tags: American Tag; Painterly Tags (True Love) by KI Memories

Metal Items: Colored Flower Brads and Colored Mini Brads by Making Memories

Ribbons: Offray, Beaux Regards, Doodlebug Design, May Arts and others: Local Craft Store

Adhesives: Art Accentz Terrifically Tacky Tape by Provo Craft

Other: Silk Flowers

Tools: Fantastix Coloring Tool Brush Point by Tsukineko, or Marker; Paper Cutter; Pinking Shears by Mundial

tip! These pre-made cards are so easy to use and are real time savers!

A Friend Hugs Your Heart

Dawne Renee Pitts

instructions

1. Stamp Flower Girl on the bottom right of the front of the card. Color the flowers with the Fantastix Coloring Tool Brush Point.

2. Cut a length of ribbon slightly wider than the card and attach along the top of the pocket. Attach three silk flowers with three brads. Pink the ends of the ribbon that hang over the edges of the card.

3. Stamp a rectangle using the faux postage stamp on the lime green cardstock and cut out; stamp "A friend" inside the rectangle and attach to the front of the card.

4. Cover three-fourths of the tag insert with various ribbons.

5. Stamp "Hugs" on four individual tags using the Mara-Mi alphabet set. Attach tags so they show when the tag is inserted in the card. Put a colored brad in each tag.

6. Stamp "your" on the ribbon using the StazOn ink.

7. Attach the KI Memories tag with a lime green mini brad.

8. Cut four pieces of ribbon and attach to the top of the tag.

Out of this World

Dawne Renee Pitts

materials

Rubber Stamps: Mod Car, Asterisk Belt, Small Asterisk and Large Asterisk by The Cat's Pajamas Rubber Stamp Company

Pigment Inkpads: Brilliance (Graphite Black) by Tsukineko; ColorBox (Orange and Fresh Green) Cat's Eye by Clearsnap

Dye Inkpads: ColorBox (Charcoal) Fluid Chalk by Clearsnap

Papers: Orange, Turquoise and Lime Green Cardstock

Rub-On Letters: All Mixed Up Expressions in Bubblegum (Small), Marmalade (Large) and Limeade (Large) by Doodlebug Design

Ribbons and Fibers: Cupcake Stitched Grosgrain Ribbon by Doodlebug Design and May Arts; Turquoise Fibers by Awesome Albums: Local Craft Store

Adhesives: Art Accentz Terrifically Tacky Tape by Provo Craft; Pop Dots by All Night Media/Plaid, or Foam Tape; Glue Dots by Glue Dots International

Other: Black Buttons

Tools: Paper Cutter; Pinking Shears by Fiskars

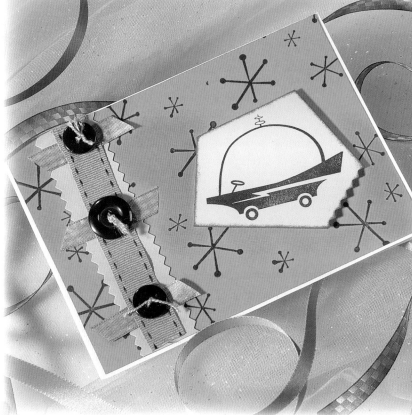

instructions

1. Cut orange background cardstock, stamp with the asterisk stamp and adhere to card front.

2. Stamp Mod Car on lime green cardstock and cut out in a geometric pattern. Pink random edge and ink with charcoal chalk ink. Adhere to card front using Pop Dots.

3. Cut a strip of turquoise cardstock and pink edges.

4. Cut a piece of the Doodlebug grosgrain ribbon and use turquoise fibers to sew on black buttons.

5. Cut three small snippets of May Arts gingham ribbon. Adhere with Glue Dots as shown (lining up with buttons, edges peeking out at sides).

6. Tape prepared purple ribbon piece and turquoise cardstock strip on card front.

7. Using the Doodlebug rub-ons, spell out your sentiment on white cardstock; mix colors to add whimsy.

8. Cut out each word and rub edges with orange and green inks; mount on turquoise cardstock, pink edge as shown. Attach to inside of card.

materials

Rubber Stamps: Alphabet Collage Set by Turtle Press

Papers: Textured Cardstock by DieCuts With A View, Multi Squares on White and Beach Ball Stripes by Scenic Route

Dye Inkpads: Distress Ink by Tim Holtz (Fired Brick) by Ranger Industries

Ribbons: May Arts; Gingham Tangerine Bumblebee, Grosgrain Limeade and Citrus Squeeze by Doodlebug Design: Local Craft Store

Other: Buttons

Adhesives: Glue Dots and Glue Lines by Glue Dots International

Tools: Stapler; Regular and/or Colored Staples; Pinking Shears by Mundial; 12-Inch Paper Cutter by Fiskars

Hello to a Special Friend
Nikki Cleary

tip! Try colored staples — they add sparkle to your creation!

instructions

1. Cut orange cardstock. Cut blue cardstock 1/4" smaller and adhere together with a glue stick or Glue Dots.

2. Cut equal lengths of both patterned papers and glue wrong sides together to form paper for card.

3. Fold as shown and burnish with a bone folder making front flap of card shorter then back. Glue to orange and blue layered cardstock.

4. Cut orange cardstock and stamp "Hello". Staple ribbons and adhere to inside with Glue Dots.

5. Cut another piece of orange cardstock and stamp "Friend" on it; pink the edges and use regular or colored staples to add ribbons. Adhere to front with Glue Dots.

6. Wrap polka-dotted ribbon around right side of card front with Glue Line. Tie ribbon through button and adhere with Glue Dots.

You Are My Sunshine

Dawne Renee Pitts

materials

Rubber Stamps: Playful Alphabet, Printers Type, Good Alphabets and Stitched Border by Hero Arts

Pigment Inkpads: ColorBox (Charcoal) Fluid Chalk by Clearsnap-Memories (Black) by Stewart Superior

Hybrid Inkpads: Palette Metallics (Emerald Gloss) Hybrid by Stewart Superior

Papers: Gatefold Card by DieCuts with a View; Summer Dot Paper by KI Memories; White Cardstock: Local Craft Store

Rub-On Letters: Scrapworks, Doodlebug Design and Making Memories

Metal Items: Mini Colored Brads by Making Memories; Eyelets by Doodlebug Design:

Ribbons: May Arts, Doodlebug Design, Beaux Regards and Offray: Local Craft Store

Adhesives: Art Accentz Terrifically Tacky Tape by Provo Craft

Tools: Circle Punch by Marvy Uchida

instructions

1. Punch out circle from KI Memories patterned paper. Ink edges with charcoal ink. Cut circle in half.

2. Attach the half circles to each side of the card so that the circle is complete when the card is closed.

3. Cut various ribbons and adhere to represent the rays of the sun.

4. Stamp the Hero Arts Stitched Border stamp on white cardstock.

5. Stamp the words "You are my" using a mixture of the Hampton Art stamps.

6. Using various colors of rub-ons, finish the sentiment "sunshine" and cut it into a rectangle.

7. Sew together two pieces of wide ribbon and attach the white cardstock sentiment with colored brads.

8. Set two eyelets in the front of the card and tie the card together using coordinating ribbon.

You're Terrific
Dawne Renee Pitts

materials

Rubber Stamps: "xoxo" Stamp by Bella Geste for Hampton Art

Hybrid Inkpads: Palette Hybrid (Claret) by Stewart Superior

Papers: Textured Cardstock by DieCuts with a View; Patterned Papers by Uptown Collection by Close to My Heart

Rub-on Letters: KI Memories

Tags: Small Jewelry Tag by American Tag or at Local Craft Store; "Made with Love & Kisses" Tag: Local Craft Store

Metal Items: Colored Staples by Making Memories; Colored Safety Pin by Li'l Davis Designs; Dotlets by Doodlebug Design

Ribbons: J. Caroline Creative and Hugs & Kisses Ribbon: Local Craft Store; Green Rick Rack: Local Craft or Fabric Store

Fabrics: Purple Felt, Tulle and Quilt Binding (various colors): Local Fabric Store

Adhesives: Art Accentz Terrifically Tacky Tape by Provo Craft

Other: Vintage Button; Carpet Thread

Tools: Pinking Shears by Mundial; Sewing Machine

instructions

1. Trim a 12" x 12" piece of turquoise textured cardstock to 11" x 12" and score to make the card base. Cut a piece of the patterned paper slightly smaller than 6" x 11".

2. Sew a piece of purple felt to the patterned paper. Cut a length of quilt binding and pink one end. Sew it to the felt to use as the flower stem.

3. Sew the "made with love" tag to the bottom left of the purple felt.

4. Cut circles of various shades of tulle; sew them together in the middle, gathering them up as you sew. Attach vintage button as flower center, using carpet thread for added strength. Using pinking shears, randomly snip into the "flower" and fluff to give it dimension. (Use regular scissors to "texturize" the flower.) Sew the flower to the felt.

5. Cut a piece of green rick rack and pin it to the flower stem; stamp a small jewelry tag with "xoxo" and attach.

6. Cut a piece of striped ribbon and pink the ends. Attach across the top right corner of the purple felt; cross it with a piece of the "hugs & kisses" ribbon. Attach using Making Memories colored staples, stapling to make an "x".

7. Adhere entire piece to the front of the card with adhesive and Dotlets.

8. For the inside sentiment, cut a piece of textured cardstock to approximately 9" x 4"; randomly pink edges to add whimsy.

9. Use rub-on letters to add the sentiment to the patterned paper and adhere it to the pink cardstock. Add colored Dotlets.

tip! This card is larger than normal, so it would require extra postage and padding to mail, but it delivers an extra special message!

Friend

Kelly Lunceford

materials

Rubber Stamps: "Love without End" Stamp Set by Stampin' Up!

Dye Inkpads: Marvy Matchables (Turquoise, Pink and Light Purple) by Marvy Uchida

Papers: White, Turquoise, Pink and Rose Cardstock: Local Craft Store

Ribbons: Orchid Grosgrain Ribbon: Local Craft Store

Adhesives: Glue Stick; Foam Tape

Tools: Paper Cutter; Scissors by Fiskars; Rectangle Punch by Fiskars; 1/4-Inch Hole Punch by EK Success

Other: Compass; Pencil

instructions

1. Cut a piece of purple cardstock 5" x 10". Fold in half to create a 5" x 5" card.

2. Cut three squares of cardstock, one each of rose, pink and turquoise. Stamp a different image on each piece with coordinating ink.

3. Stagger squares and attach to a piece of white cardstock, mat on pink cardstock and attach to card.

4. Stamp flower image, outline and center onto white cardstock. Using a compass, center flower image and draw a circle around it. Pull compass out slightly and draw another circle onto turquoise cardstock, cut out and adhere stamped flower image on top with glue stick.

5. Punch rectangles on each side and tie ribbon through each hole. Attach circle to card with foam tape.

6. Stamp the word "friend" three times, once with each color of ink. Punch out letters to spell "friend" in alternating colors. Attach to card with glue stick.

7. Stamp flower outline image randomly over the inside of card in turquoise ink.

8. To complete the inside of the card, stamp "Love" phrase with pink ink onto white cardstock. Mat onto turquoise, then pink, then a larger piece of white. Leave enough space to stamp "friend" at the bottom.

Hello Friend

Amy Wellenstein

materials

Rubber Stamps: Bordered Daisy by Uptown Design Company; Hipster Lower Case Alphabet Stamps by Renaé Lindgren for Creative Imaginations; Polka Dots by Hot Potatoes

Pigment Inkpads: VersaMagic by Tsukineko

Dye Inkpads: Archival Ink (Carnation Pink and Aqua) by Ranger Industries

Papers: Teal and White Cardstock: Local Craft Store; Frenzy Ditty Dots by Paper Fever; Ave Coral Soho Stripe (Dots) by Making Memories

Ribbons: Plaid and Fuchsia Ribbon by May Arts; Rick Rack (Bubblegum and Swimming Pool) by Doodlebug Design; Stitched Edge Ribbon (Teal and Orange): Local Craft Store

Adhesives: Double-Stick Tape; The Ultimate! Glue by Crafter's Pick; Glue Dots and Glue Lines by Glue Dots International; Xyron

Other: Waxed Linen Cord (Black); Small Green Button

Tools: Paper Cutter

instructions

1. Use Xyron to adhere patterned paper to white cardstock for stability.

2. Use double-stick tape and glue to adhere coordinating ribbons and rick rack to the patterned panel.

3. Stamp "Dots" on a square of teal cardstock using VersaMagic ink.

4. Stamp "Bordered Daisy" on a square of white cardstock using Carnation Pink ink.

5. Layer together these stamped panels and a square of orange patterned paper and adhere to the ribbon panel using Glue Lines.

6. Adhere the embellished panel to a teal card, add button with Glue Dots.

7. Stamp "HELLO FRIEND" on a strip of patterned paper using aqua ink. Adhere to the inside of the card.

8. Further embellish the inside of the card with coordinating strips of decorative paper.

Chapter 3 · Valentine's Day

On this special day of hearts and flowers, I think back to the valentine cards we learned to make in grade school. Remember those days? Using scissors, glue and lots of love, we made magic with construction paper, doilies and crayons. I still have wonderful memories of racing home with anticipation to give my heartfelt creation to my parents.

In this chapter, you'll learn some new twists on that lovely old concept. You may not even want to wait for Valentine's Day! These handmade expressions of love are sure to surprise and delight whoever receives them, any time of year.

You Make My Heart Go Pitty-Pat

Dawne Renee Pitts

materials

Rubber Stamps: Signature Lowercase Alphabet by Hero Arts

Dye Inkpads: Memories (Black) by Stewart Superior

Papers: Warm Hearted and Crazy for You Papers by KI Memories; Pieces of Me, True Love Collection and Textured Cardstock by Bazzill Basics from the Doodlebug Bubblegum Trio

Metal Items: Dotlets by Doodlebug Design

Ribbons: May Arts, Beaux Regards, Offray and others: Local Craft Store

Adhesives: Art Accentz Terrifically Tacky Tape by Provo Craft

Tools: Paper Cutter; Needle and Thread; Pinking Shears by Mundial

instructions

1. Using the Doodlebug Bubblegum cardstock, cut and fold bright pink card.

2. Cut out a piece of the KI Memories Warm Hearted paper and pink all edges. Attach to front of card using Dotlets.

3. Cut out a heart shape from spare cardstock; apply a small amount of tape to center of the heart.

4. Cover the heart using various pink and red ribbons, allowing edges to hang over.

5. Hand- or machine-stitch around the edges of the heart and pink all around the heart.

6. Attach the heart to the front of the card.

7. Cut out another piece of the KI Memories Warm Hearted paper and pink around the entire piece.

8. Stamp sentiment on the KI Memories paper.

9. Attach to the inside of the card with the Dotlets.

10. Cut out a piece of the KI memories Crazy for You paper and attach to inside of card.

I Adore You

Dawne Renee Pitts

materials

Rubber Stamps: Groovy Heart and Love Wire Stamps by Stampendous; Big Scroll Frame by The Cat's Pajamas Rubber Stamp Company; Classic Upper and Lower Case Alphabet Stamps by Hero Arts

Hybrid Inkpads: Palette Hybrid (Claret) by Stewart Superior

Papers: Coral Cardstock: Local Craft Store

Tags: Heart Tag by Lost Art Treasures by American Tag

Metal Items: Dotlet by Doodlebug Design

Fabrics: Tulle: Local Craft or Fabric Store

Adhesives: Pop Up Glue Dots by Glue Dots International; Art Accentz Terrifically Tacky Tape by Provo Craft

Other: Safety Pin; Heart Charm

Tools: Paper Cutter; Pinking Shears by Mundial

instructions

1. Cut and fold coral cardstock to make card; pink bottom of the front of the card.

2. On a separate sheet of paper, stamp the Groovy Heart, Love Wire and Big Scroll Frame, using Claret ink.

3. Cut out the three stamped images; ink around the edges of each with Claret ink.

4. Attach the Love Wire stamp along the bottom of the card. Attach the heart tag using the Dotlet.

5. Attach the Groovy Heart to the front of the card using the Pop Up Glue Dots.

6. Stamp your sentiment inside the Big Scroll frame, replacing the "O" in adore with a heart from the Hero Arts set.

7. Cut lengths of magenta and coral tulle and tie across the top of the card. Fan out the bows for fullness. Attach the "love" charm using a safety pin through the knot of the bow.

tip! Tulle is a fun and inexpensive way to add something extra to your cards. It comes in so many wonderful colors!

Love to You
Lindsay Haglund

materials

Rubber Stamps: Big Heart by Stampotique Originals; Happy Valentine's Day by PSX

Dye Inkpads: Memories (Cherry Red) by Stewart Superior

Papers: Printed Red Words by 7gypsies; Red and Cream Cardstock: Local Craft Store; White Iron-On Adhesive Letters (LOVE) by SEI

Ribbons: Local Craft Store

Fabrics: Red Tulle: Local Craft or Fabric Store

Buttons: Small Red Buttons by Making Memories

Adhesives: Xyron

Tools: Paper Cutter

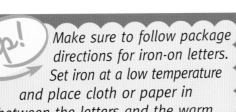
tip! Make sure to follow package directions for iron-on letters. Set iron at a low temperature and place cloth or paper in between the letters and the warm iron. Increase heat on iron only as needed to allow for adhesion.

instructions

1. Cut and fold red cardstock to make card.
2. Cut smaller pieces of cream and printed red word paper; adhere using Xyron adhesive as shown to red card.
3. Cut red and white polka-dotted ribbon and adhere to card; trim edges flush.
4. Adhere LOVE iron-on letters to ribbon as shown.
5. Snip ribbon ends at an angle and attach to card using Xyron adhesive.s
6. Stamp "Happy Valentine's Day" inside and adhere small bow to the inside of the card.
7. Twist small strips of red tulle and attach with Glue Dots. Add small red buttons on top of the twists with Glue Dots as shown.
8. Finish off by cutting a piece of ribbon to tie into bow on the side of the card.

materials

Rubber Stamps: Heart Tiles By Magenta; Love by PrintWorks

Pigment Inkpads: VersaFine (Onyx Black) by Tsukineko

Papers: Black and White Cardstock: Local Craft Store; Metro Pink Polka Dots Paper by Made to Match by American Crafts

Markers: Light Blue and Pink by Marvy Uchida

Ribbons: Local Craft Store

Adhesives: Glue Stick; Xyron; Pop Up Glue Dots and Mini Glue Dots by Glue Dots International; Double Stick-Tape

Other: White Buttons

Tools: Paper Cutter; Scissors; Circle Punch by Marvy Uchida; Sandpaper

Heart Tiles Valentine

Amy Wellenstein

instructions

1. Stamp Heart Tiles on white cardstock using ink. Color with markers and cut the tiles apart.

2. Layer the tiles on black and white cardstock, then mount on a rectangular black cardstock panel using Glue Dots.

3. Adhere small white buttons in the corners using Mini Glue Dots.

4. Trim a panel of pink polka dot paper to fit on the front of a folded black card.

5. Sand the edges of the polka dot panel.

6. Adhere several coordinating ribbons to the pink panel using Xyron adhesive; trim ends flush with panel.

7. Layer the stamped panel and the ribbon panel on the black card.

8. Stamp "Love" on pink polka dot paper using black ink.

9. Use a large circle punch to punch out the stamped sentiment.

10. Adhere the circle and a piece of coordinating ribbon to the inside of the card.

Hot For You Valentine Card

Amy Wellenstein

materials

Rubber Stamps: Carol's Flower and Dots by Stampotique Originals; Hot For You by Hot Potatoes

Pigment Inkpads: VersaMark (Watermark) and VersaFine (Onyx Black) by Tsukineko

Dye Inkpads: Archival (Crimson) by Ranger Industries

Papers: Hot Pink and Smooth White Cardstock: Local Craft Store; Black Cardstock by Bazzill Basics; Cotton Candy from Lollipop Shoppe by Basic Grey

Chalks: Yellow and Hot Pink Chalks by Deluxe Designs

Ribbons: Local Craft Store

Adhesives: Glue Stick; Mini Glue Dots by Glue Dots International; Xyron

Tools: Xacto Knife; Cutting Mat; Clear Ruler; Bone Folder

Other: Clear Buttons

tip! Cutting windows on the front of a card is a great way to use the sentiment on the inside as a design element.

instructions

1. Cut and fold black cardstock to make card. Cut out a heart from hot pink cardstock; trim a small window out of the heart.

2. Stamp the heart with "Carol's Flower" using Crimson ink.

3. Use glue stick to adhere the stamped heart to the front of black card.

4. Cut a window through the front of black card.

5. Stamp "Dots" on white cardstock using VersaMark ink.

6. Let the ink dry for approximately two minutes, then highlight with yellow and pink chalks.

7. Stamp "hot for you" over the dots using black ink.

8. Adhere the stamped panel to inside of card (positioning it so that the sentiment can be read through the window).

9. Adhere narrow pink ribbon to right edge of card using Xyron adhesive.

10. Use Mini Glue Dots to attach three clear buttons to the lower right corner.

11. Adhere a strip of striped paper to right edge of inside of card (for a decorative extension that can be seen when the card is closed).

12. Tie a sheer pink ribbon to left edge of card.

Valentine Cards

by Dawne Renee Pitts • Concept by Kim Henkel

materials

Rubber Stamps: Heart Bullseye by Savvy Stamps; Whoop-dee-do by Hampton Art; "xoxo" by Hampton Art; 2 Hugs and Kiss by PSX; Lips by PSX; "I..u..us…" by Magenta

Dye Inkpads: Memories (Black) by Stewart Superior

Hybrid Inkpads: Palette Hybrid (Claret and L'Amour Red) by Stewart Superior

Papers: Pink, Melon, Red and Purple Cardstock: Local Craft Store; Pink Ticket: Local Office Supply

Tags: Local Craft Store

Metal Items: Safety Pins

Ribbons: Assorted Ribbons and Rick Rack: Local Craft Store

Fabrics: Tulle (assorted colors): Local Fabric Store

Adhesives: Glue Stick or Hermafix Tabs

Other: Silk Flower

instructions

1. Cut and fold a card of desired size from colored cardstock.

2. Use a few fun valentine images stamped in red, purple or black inks.

3. Adorn with bows made from tulle, silk or paper flowers, different shaped tags, ribbons, rick rack, charms, tickets and safety pins as shown in photo.

tip! These are quick and simple to do! You can also make the same type of cards for other holidays and special occasions throughout the year such as Christmas, wedding showers, birthday parties, graduation, new baby and more!

Chapter 4 · Gift Cards

Yes! Gift Cards! They're great for surprising your friends and family with gift certificates, cards, coupons or tickets. Anyone, anytime will appreciate your thoughtful purchase and will treasure the handmade card it came in. Use your imagination to come up with gift ideas. Here are a few to get you started:

* Gift card to the local craft store for a girlfriend

* Coupon for the carwash for your husband

* Tickets to a sports event for any sports fan

* Gift certificate to a pizza parlor for teens

* Bus, train or airplane ticket for your parents

* Tickets to the theatre, opera or symphony for friends

* Gift certificate to a pet store for a child's birthday

* Coupon for ice cream for kids of all ages

* Gift card to Starbucks for anyone

And who wouldn't love to be treated to a meal at their favorite restaurant, a book from their local bookstore, or anything they fancy from a department store? These cards are fun to make, they're gifts that keep on giving, and the possibilities are endless!

Wish Big

Dawne Renee Pitts

materials

Rubber Stamps: Wish Big by PSX

Pigment Inkpads: Colorbox (Dark Brown) Fluid Chalk by Clearsnap

Dye Inkpads: Memories (Black) by Stewart Superior

Papers: Frenzy Ditty Dots and Frenzy Pinstripes by Paperfever

Tags: Two Oversized Tags by American Tag

Ribbons: May Arts and others: Local Craft Store

Metal Items: Eyelets and Dotlets by Doodlebug Design

Adhesives: Art Accentz Terrifically Tacky Tape by Provo Craft

Tools: Paper Cutter; Pinking Shears by Mundial; Bone Folder; Eyelet Setter

4U With Love

Dawne Renee Pitts

materials

Rubber Stamps: Mara-Mi Alphabet Set by Hampton Art; Small Flower Stamp from the Classic Lowercase Alphabet Set by Hero Arts

Pigment Inkpads: ColorBox (Charcoal) Fluid Chalk by Clearsnap; ColorBox (Peony) by Clearsnap

Dye Inkpads: Memories (Black) by Stewart Superior

Papers: Stylin' Stripes by Dena Designs for Creative Imaginations; Dots & Daisies Paper by Doodlebug Design; Lime Green and Hot Pink Cardstock: Local Craft Store

Tags: Large Square Tag: Local Craft Store or Office Supply

Metal Items: Flower Brads by Making Memories

Ribbons: Various Ribbons and Rick Rack: Local Craft Store

Adhesives: Art Accentz Terrifically Tacky Tape by Provo Craft

Other: Embroidery Thread

Tools: Paper Cutter; Stencils; Xacto Knife and Glass Mat

instructions

1. Cut one tag to make a pocket, depending on the size of your gift card.
2. Cover with patterned paper and ink the edges with brown ink.
3. Cut patterned papers to fit a whole tag, ink edges and attach pocket.
4. Stamp image on lime green cardstock and attach to dark brown cardstock. Pink sides of brown cardstock. Attach to front of pocket at a slight angle.
5. Cut out rectangular strip of lime green cardstock and pink edges. Fold over top of tag in center and adhere. Punch hole in top and set two colorful eyelets. Run a five-inch snippet of wide ribbon through eyelets and double-knot. Pink edges of ribbon.
6. Set eyelets at top of pocket on each side to thread ribbon through. Set Dotlets down the side of the card.

tip! The key to good Xacto work is a very sharp blade, and cutting on a glass mat - oh, and the three P's: Practice, practice and practice!

instructions

1. Cover a large square tag with striped paper.
2. Trace stencils onto lime green cardstock and cut out using Xacto knife.
3. Stamp flowers on the stencils and back with Doodlebug floral paper.
4. Attach the stencils to the hot pink cardstock, leaving a small border on all sides; pink the ends and attach to the card to make a pocket.
5. Attach the rick rack and flower brads to the top of the pocket.
6. Stamp "with love" using the Mara-Mi alphabet stamps onto the hot pink cardstock. Cut out the words, pinking one end of each word; ink the edges.
7. Attach the "with" and "love" to the center of the two stencils.
8. Sew bits of ribbon to the top of the card, attaching them with black buttons of various sizes; use colorful embroidery thread to attach the buttons.

Cup of Happy

Dawne Renee Pitts

tip! Using ColorBox Cat's Eye Inkpads makes inking the edges of your papers easier!

materials

Rubber Stamps: Coffee by Stampa Rosa; Coffee Cup by Wordsworth

Pigment Inkpads: ColorBox (Charcoal and Cyan) by Clearsnap; Brilliance (Graphite Black) by Tsukineko

Embossing Powders: Gold Ultra Thick Embossing Enamel (UTEE) by Suze Weinberg

Papers: Colorful Stripe by KI Memories; Frenzy Ring-a-Ding by Paperfever; Pink and Turquoise Cardstock: Local Craft Store

Computer Fonts: Airplane by Two Peas in a Bucket

Alphabet Stickers: Sarah Script Monograms by American Crafts

Metal Items: Swimming Pool Eyelets by Doodlebug Design

Ribbons: May Arts: Local Craft Store

Adhesives: Pop Dots by All Night Media/Plaid; Art Accentz Terrifically Tacky Tape by Provo Craft

Tools: Paper Cutter; Pinking Shears by Fiskars; Bone Folder

instructions

1. Cut and fold turquoise cardstock to make card. Ink edges of front and inside of card with ColorBox Cyan ink.

2. Cut a block of KI Memories striped paper to fit the front and inside of card; ink edges and adhere

3. Cut a smaller square of the Paperfever paper, ink edges and adhere to the front of the card.

4. Stamp coffee stamp onto pink cardstock and emboss. Cut out the image.

5. Cut an oblong piece of turquoise cardstock and pink edges. Adhere the small coffee cup image with Pop Dots. Adhere both pieces to the front of the card.

6. Make a pocket out of pink cardstock and attach a small strip of the Paperfever paper to the top of the pocket. Ink all edges and adhere to the bottom inside of the card.

7. Stamp the small Wordsworth coffee cup stamp to the bottom right corner of the pocket.

8. Cut a piece of turquoise cardstock and pink edges. Attach to the pocket.

9. Print out phrase onto pink cardstock and cut out. Ink edges and attach to the turquoise cardstock piece.

10. Set eyelets and thread ribbon through, tying in a bow.

tip! Change stamp images and insert a check for a fabulous graduation or birthday gift.

4U Gift Card

Amy Wellenstein

materials

Rubber Stamps: Retro Star and Times New Roman Alphabet/Number Set by Hot Potatoes

Pigment Inkpads: VersaMagic by Tsukineko

Dye Inkpads: Impress (Pansy) by Tsukineko

Papers: Black and White Cardstock: Local Craft Store

Ribbons: Lime Green Satin Ribbon by Europa at Local Craft Store; Multicolored Stripe and Aqua Dot Ribbons by Offray; Green Shimmer and Purple Ribbons by May Arts; Teal Grosgrain Ribbon and Teal Ribbon with Lime Stitching on Edges: Local Craft Store

Adhesives: The Ultimate! Glue by Crafter's Pick; Glue Lines by Glue Dots International; Xyron; PeelnStick Double-Stick Tape Sheets by Therm O Web; Double-Stick Tape

Other: Lime Green Button; Rhinestone; Green Coin Envelope

Tools: Paper Cutter; Rotary Cutter by Fiskars

instructions

1. Trim a PeelnStick double-stick tape sheet to approximately 4.25" x 9".

2. Remove one side of the liner and adhere the sheet to a piece of white cardstock (of the same size).

3. Remove the other liner to expose the other adhesive side of the double-stick tape sheet.

4. Adhere rows of coordinating ribbons to the sticky side of the sheet. Burnish well.

5. Cut two squares (approximately 4.25" squares) from the sheet of ribbons.

6. Cut each of the squares in half diagonally.

7. Apply Xyron adhesive to the back of all four ribbon triangles.

8. Adhere the triangles to a piece of white cardstock to form a square.

9. Layer the embellished panel on a folded black card.

10. Stamp "retro star" on a square of white cardstock using pansy ink.

11. Layer on black cardstock and adhere to the front of the card using Glue Lines.

12. Embellish the stamped panel with a rhinestone (using a green button as a "bezel").

13. For the inside of the card, trim the end off of a coordinating green coin envelope.

14. Stamp the "retro star" on the envelope using VersaMagic ink.

15. Stamp "4U" on the envelope using pansy ink.

16. Use double-stick tape to adhere a piece of ribbon around the end of the envelope. Tape the envelope to the inside of the card.

17. Insert a gift card into the envelope.

Chapter 5 · St. Patrick's Day

Like a pot of gold at the end of a rainbow, this card is sure to please. And you don't need the luck of the Irish to make it! Just get your hands on everything GREEN. The coordinating papers, ribbons, inks and whimsical alphabet stamps and computer fonts used here will put a twinkle in anyone's eye.

Pinch Me

Dawne Renee Pitts

materials

Rubber Stamps: Tall Alphabet by Stampotique; Good Luck Stamp by Stampcraft

Hybrid Inkpads: Palette Hybrid (Chartreuse) by Stewart Superior

Papers: Bright Green Cardstock: Local Craft Store

Computer Fonts: Fat Frog by Two Peas in a Bucket

Metal Items: Green Staples by Making Memories

Ribbons: Offray, Beaux Regards, Doodlebug Design and May Arts: Local Craft Store

Tools: Paper Cutter; Stapler; Hammer

instructions

1. Use your computer to write and print out your sentiment on white cardstock.

2. Cut out the sentiment and add "Green" with Tall Alphabet stamp set.

3. Ink around the edges of both journaling boxes.

4. Staple various pieces of green ribbons around the sentiment box for the front of the card. Turn the block over and lightly hammer the staples closed for stability.

5. Once you've finished stapling the ribbons on the sentiment box, determine how big you want your card to be and cut it out of bright green cardstock.

6. Staple the sentiment blocks on the cover and inside of the card.

tip! This card literally takes 15 minutes to make. Save every little snip of ribbon, and keep it in a small jar. These sorts of cards are such a fun way to use those snips, and the colored staples add a little sparkle and a finishing touch. No adhesive was used at all on this card.... just staples!

but you can pinch me anyway!

Happy St. Patrick's Day!

Hippity Hoppity Happy Easter

Dawne Renee Pitts

materials

Rubber Stamps: Flower Bunny by Savvy Stamps; Mara-Mi Alphabet Set by Hampton Art; Mod Squares Alphabet by Stampendous

Dye Inkpads: Memories (Midnight Blue) by Stewart Superior

Papers: Textured Cardstock by Bazzill Basics from the Doodlebug Limeade Trio and Bubblegum Trio; White Cardstock: Local Craft Store

Metal Items: Colored Brads by Making Memories; Colored Staples by Making Memories

Ribbons: Offray, Beaux Regards and May Arts: Local Craft Store

Adhesives: Glue Dots by Glue Dots International; Glue Stick

Tools: Paper Cutter

instructions

1. Cut limeade cardstock to make card.

2. Stamp the bunny onto the Bubblegum cardstock.

3. Cut a piece of white cardstock smaller than the card front. Attach the piece of Bubblegum paper with the bunny stamped on it to the center of the white cardstock.

4. Measure out pieces of ribbons to make a frame around the bunny. Cover entire piece of white cardstock with ribbons. Use Glue Dots to secure the ribbons in place.

5. Attach the colored brads randomly, securing pieces of the ribbon. Attach the ribbon frame to the Limeade cardstock using the four colored flower brads.

6. Stamp the words "Hippity," "Hoppity," and "Happy" on the Bubblegum cardstock and cut out in strips. Attach ribbon bits to the end of each strip using a colored staple. Adhere to inside.

7. Stamp the word "Easter" using the Mod Squares Alphabet. Cut out each word and glue to inside of card.

Chapter 6 · Easter

*Think bunnies, flowers, eggs and
baskets and yummy colors of ribbons! Easter
is a great time to go all out with COLOR, from glorious
bursts of brilliant shades to touchably soft pastels. Fill your basket
with pinks, purples, blues, greens, yellows and oranges and enjoy making these
beautiful Easter cards for the special people in your life.*

Chapter 7 · Mother's Day

What mother wouldn't LOVE a handmade card for Mother's Day? Let your creation take her back to the "good old days," when you eagerly crafted cards for her in grade school. Look for stamps that express your special message, or handwrite or print your inside sentiment using downloadable fonts. No matter your choice, your card is sure to spell "cherish."

You're the Greatest Mom

Nikki Cleary

materials

Rubber Stamps: Friendly Messages and Dream Text by Stampendous; Loopy Letters by EK Success

Hybrid Inkpads: Hybrid Palette (Claret) by Stewart Superior

Papers: Plum Harlequin Latch Card by Making Memories; Textured Olive Green Cardstock and Printed Paper by DieCuts with a View

Ribbons: May Arts: Local Craft Store

Metal Items: Colored Staples by Making Memories

Adhesives: Glue Dots by Glue Dots International

Other: Buttons

Tools: Paper Cutter; Stapler; Large, Medium and Small Square Punches by Marvy Uchida

instructions

1. Use large square punch to make three olive green squares and adhere with Glue Dots.

2. Use medium square punch to make three patterned paper squares and adhere to the green squares with Glue Dots.

3. Cut ribbon to fold over and adhere to flap of card with a staple.

4. Adhere the three buttons with Glue Dots.

5. Take the white insert of the card and stamp "have a great day."

6. Use small square punch and punch out three squares of olive green cardstock. Stamp "M" "O" "M" on squares. Adhere stamped squares to the tag insert with Glue Dots.

7. Cut snippet of ribbon, fold and adhere to the top of the tag insert. Add button with Glue Dot.

There's No Other Like My Mother

Amy Wellenstein

materials

Rubber Stamps: Dots Spotlight by Paper Inspirations; Magnetic Alphabet Stamps (Providence) By Making Memories; Face Stamp: Local Craft Store

Dye Inkpads: Memories (Black) Inkpad: Stewart Superior; Archival (Carnation and Aqua) by Ranger Industries

Papers: Green Matchbook Card by Making Memories; White, Pink, and Chartreuse Cardstock: Local Craft Store; Tutti Frutti by Lollipop Shoppe by Basic Grey

Metal Items: Mini Silver Brad and Flower Brads (Watercolor Brite) by Making Memories

Ribbons: Local Craft or Fabric Store

Adhesives: Double-Stick Tape

Tools: Paper Cutter; Sandpaper

tip! Sand your papers lightly for added texture or a "distressed" look.

instructions

1. Stamp face on white cardstock using aqua ink.

2. Mask face (stamp another image, cut it out and cover up the first image you stamped so it won't show a second stamped image) and over-stamp with Dots using Carnation ink.

3. Layer stamped panel on pink cardstock, then on floral patterned paper, sand lightly.

4. Use double-stick tape to adhere pink and aqua ribbons down the left side of the floral panel.

5. Attach pink flower brads to the panel.

6. Adhere the panel to a green matchbook card.

7. Use double-stick tape to adhere ribbons and a strip of cardstock across the bottom of the card; insert brad.

8. For the inside of the card, stamp "Theres no other Like my Mother" on a scrap of white cardstock using black ink.

9. Cut out the words and adhere to a pink panel. Embellish the panel with a strip of coordinating paper and adhere to inside of card.

Happily Ever After

Dawne Renee Pitts

tip! The same beautiful design can be used for a birthday card by using brightly colored tulle and lace along with an inside birthday sentiment.

materials

Rubber Stamps: Sangria Background by Hampton Art; Label Cube by Postmodern Design; Happily Ever After by Catslife Press

Hybrid Inkpads: Palette Metallics Hybrid (Luminous Periwinkle) by Stewart Superior

Papers: White Cardstock

Metal Items: White Eyelets: Local Craft Store

Ribbons and Lace: Local Craft Store

Fabrics: White Tulle: Local Craft or Fabric Store

Other: Small Bow with Pearl

Adhesives: Glue Dots by Glue Dots International; Art Accentz Terrifically Tacky Tape by Provo Craft

instructions

1. Cut and fold card from white cardstock.

2. Cut out three rectangles from a separate sheet of heavy white cardstock, in graduating sizes, larger to smaller, to emulate the cake tiers.

3. Cover each rectangle of cardstock with ribbons and lace as shown in photo.

4. Use Glue Dots to attach the three rectangles to the card to form a wedding cake.

5. In the upper left-hand corner, set two white eyelets at an angle.

6. Pull a long piece of white tulle through the eyelets and tie in a bow. Fan out the bow and cut the ends to desired length.

7. Stamp the Sangria background on a separate piece of white cardstock. Cut out a heart and adhere it to the top of the wedding cake with Glue Dots.

8. Stamp the label and sentiment on a separate piece of white cardstock; cut out. Adhere message to inside of card. Add a tiny bow with pearl.

Chapter 8 · Wedding

Although you may have the majority of your wedding invitations professionally printed, you can still make cards for each member of the wedding party. What an extraordinary way to invite them to be a part of your special day or to say "thank you" for being involved! Soft organdy, ribbons and lace, beautiful silver cording and pastels send a heartfelt message in a genuine and sweet way.

Best Wishes

Kelly Lunceford

materials

Rubber Stamps: Occasionally, Sincere Salutations, All Year Cheer Set 1 and Wonderful Words II by Stampin' Up!

Dye Inkpads: Adirondack (Meadow) by Ranger Industries; Marvy Matchables (Grey) by Marvy Uchida

Papers: Moss, Peach and White Cardstock: Local Craft Store

Tags: Metal-Rimmed Tags: Local Craft Store

Metal Items: Mini Brads by Making Memories

Ribbons: Light Green, Pink, Silver and Organdy Ribbons: Local Craft Store

Adhesives: Glue Stick; Foam Tape; Scotch Tape by 3M; Mini Glue Dots by Glue Dots International

Other: Silver Cord: Local Craft Store

Tools: Paper Cutter by Fiskars; 1/16-Inch Hole Punch by Fiskars

instructions

Outside:

1. Cut a 12" x 12" piece of white cardstock in half. Fold in half to create a 6" x 6" card.

2. Attach a slightly smaller square of moss cardstock.

3. On a rectangle of white cardstock, alternate organdy ribbons and attach to the back with Scotch Tape. Wrap silver cord randomly and tie on the front where the tags will hide it.

4. Stamp wedding bell image onto a small metal-rimmed tag with Meadow ink. Cut a square of peach cardstock to nest inside larger metal-rimmed tag. Layer the two tags and attach to the rectangle with ribbons.

5. Stamp greeting onto a piece of peach cardstock with grey ink; mat with white. Punch holes and add brads. Attach to card with Mini Glue Dots.

6. Layer assembled piece onto peach cardstock and attach to card front with foam tape.

Inside:

1. Stamp "forever" onto white cardstock. Stamp "love" onto peach cardstock, add brad and attach to inside with a Mini Glue Dot.

2. Wrap a piece of light green and grey ribbon around the white cardstock and attach in the back with Scotch Tape. Add a knot of silver with a bit of silver cord and Mini Glue Dots.

3. Layer peach and moss cardstock; glue to inside of card.

BEST
wishes

Retro Happy Birthday

Amy Wellenstein

materials

Rubber Stamps: Happy Birthday Sign and Dots by Hot Potatoes; Big and Bold (Happy) by Hero Arts

Pigment Inkpads: VersaMark and VersaFine (Onyx Black) by Tsukineko

Papers: White Cardstock (super smooth): Local Craft Store or Office Supply; Black, Fuchsia and Green Cardstock: Local Craft Store; Post-it Notes by 3M; Dumbo Stripes by Sandylion Sticker Designs

Colored Pencils: Prismacolor (Pink and Yellow) by Sanford

Chalks: Deluxe Designs

Metal Items: Rhinestone Brads (Bright) SEI

Ribbons: Polka Dot Ribbons: Local Craft Store

Adhesives: Double-Stick Tape; Foam Tape

Other: Crystal Lacquer by Sakura Hobby Craft

Tools: Sizzix Machine; Oval Die Cut by Provo Craft

instructions

1. Stamp Happy Birthday Sign twice on white cardstock and once on a large Post-it Note using Onyx Black ink.

2. Trim out the "Happy" and "Birthday" from one image that was stamped on cardstock and coat them with Crystal Lacquer (these will be used to make the dimensional signs). Discard the remainder of this image and set the two signs aside to dry.

3. Trim out the image that you stamped on a Post-it to create a mask.

4. Lay the mask over the image you stamped on the other piece of white cardstock.

5. Over-stamp the panel repeatedly with the Dots stamp using VersaMark ink. (The mask will keep the Dots stamp from covering the first image you stamped.)

6. Let the VersaMark dry for approximately two minutes.

7. Apply green and yellow chalks over the VersaMark (the color will be more concentrated wherever it touches the ink).

8. Remove the mask and color the cupcake with colored pencils.

9. Layer the stamped panel on coordinating cardstock and patterned paper panels.

10. Attach rhinestone brads through the layered panel.

11. Use double-stick tape to adhere a piece of orange polka dot ribbon around the front of the card.

12. Adhere the layered panels to the front of the card.

13. Use foam tape to adhere the dimensional accents to the card.

14. For the inside of the card, use the Sizzix machine to cut an oval from yellow striped paper.

15. Stamp "Happy" on the oval using Onyx Black ink and adhere to the inside of the card at an angle.

Chapter 9 · Happy Birthday!

We all send and receive birthday cards but very rarely are they handmade. If you want to treat a close friend to a special surprise, a card you've made will do it! Your thoughtfulness will last long after the birthday is over. Use bright ribbons and vibrant papers; have fun and get crazy with color!

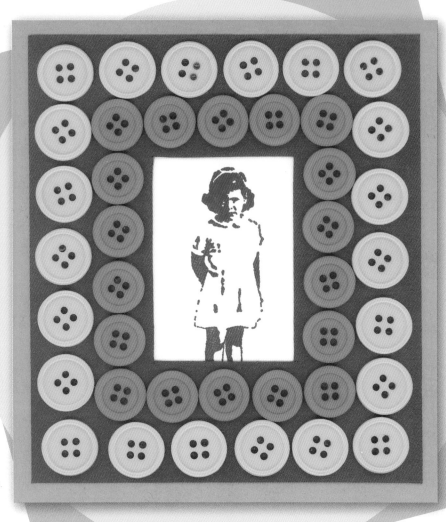

Happy Birthday Button Frame

Amy Wellenstein

materials

Rubber Stamps: Girl by Stampotique Originals; Alphabet: Local Craft Store

Papers: White, Pink and Orange Cardstock: Local Craft Store

Dye Inkpads: Impress (Cherry Pink) by Tsukineko

Adhesives: Double-Stick Tape; The Ultimate! Glue by Crafter's Pick

Other: Buttons

instructions

1. Glue yellow and orange buttons to a panel of pink cardstock to create a frame.

2. Cut out the center of the frame and mount on a folded orange card.

3. Cut the window out of the front of the card.

4. Stamp Girl on a white panel of cardstock using Cherry Pink ink.

5. Adhere the stamped panel to the inside of the card.

6. Stamp "HAPPY BIRTHDAY" across the top of the inside of the card using Cherry Pink ink.

Birthday Presents

Amy Wellenstein

materials

Rubber Stamps: Birthday Presents by Stampotique Originals; Happy Birthday by Dawn Houser for Inkadinkado Rubber Stamps

Pigment Inkpads: VersaFine (Onyx Black) by Tsukineko

Papers: Black, Pink and White Cardstock: Local Craft Store; Envy Mini Bangles by KI Memories

Colored Pencils: Prismacolor (Pink and Lime Green) by Sanford

Ribbons: Black Grosgrain, Green Dot, Green and Black Stitched Ribbons by May Arts; White Satin Ribbon: Local Craft Store

Adhesives: The Ultimate! Glue by Crafter's Pick; Glue Lines by Glue Dots International; Xyron; Double-Tack Double-Stick Tape Sheets by Grafix; Double-Stick Tape

Other: Buttons; Rhinestones

Tools: Paper Cutter; Rotary Cutter by Fiskars

instructions

1. Trim a sheet of double-stick adhesive to approximately 2 1/4" x 9".

2. Remove one side of the liner and adhere the sheet to a piece of white cardstock of the same size.

3. Remove the other liner to expose the other adhesive side of the double-stick tape sheet.

4. Adhere rows of coordinating ribbons to the sticky side of the sheet. Burnish well.

5. Cut four squares (approximately 2 1/4" square) from the sheet of ribbons.

6. Apply Xyron adhesive to the back of all four ribbon squares.

7. Adhere the squares to a piece of white cardstock to form a larger square.

8. Layer the embellished panel on a folded pink card.

9. Stamp Birthday Presents on a square of white cardstock using Onyx Black ink. Color with colored pencils.

10. Layer on black cardstock and adhere to the front of the card using Glue Lines.

11. Glue rhinestones to pink button bezels and adhere down the right side.

12. For the inside of the card, stamp "Happy Birthday" on a strip of green patterned paper using Onyx Black ink.

13. Adhere the strip to the inside of the card.

Happy, Happy Birthday!

Dawne Renee Pitts

materials

Rubber Stamps: Happy, Happy, Happy by Stampotique Originals; Bella Geste Mini Alphabet Set by Hampton Art

Dye Inkpads: Memories (Black) by Stewart Superior

Papers: Turquoise and Orange Cardstock: Local Craft Store

Metal Items: Mini Square Brads (Tropic) by Making Memories

Ribbons: Offray and May Arts: Local Craft Store

Pom Pom: Local Craft Store

Adhesives: Art Accentz Terrifically Tacky Tape by Provo Craft; Glue Dots by Glue Dots International

Tools: Paper Cutter; Corner Rounder

instructions

1. Cut out a party hat from the turquoise cardstock.

2. Attach a strip of wide colorful ribbon to the bottom of the front of the card.

3. Attach the pom pom trim to the bottom of the card using the square brads.

4. Cut strips of ribbon and attach to the top of the front of the card using the square brads.

5. Stamp the Happy stamp onto the orange cardstock using black ink. Round the corners and punch a hole in the top of the block. Tie ribbon through the hole and attach to the front of the card with Glue Dots.

6. Stamp your sentiment on a piece of orange cardstock and cut out. Attach to inside of card, tucking a couple of snips of ribbon behind it.

Birthday Princess

Dawne Renee Pitts

materials

Rubber Stamps: Queen Standing by Claudia Rose

Dye Inkpads: Memories (Black) by Stewart Superior

Papers: Bright Yellow and Bright Pink Cardstock: Local Craft Store

Computer Fonts: A Little Loopy by Two Peas in a Bucket

Metal Items: Eyelets and Dotlets by Doodlebug Design

Ribbons: Offray: Local Craft Store

Fabrics: Yellow Tulle: Local Craft or Fabric Store

Adhesives: Art Accentz Terrifically Tacky Tape by Provo Craft

Tools: Pinking Shears by Mundial

tip! Don't worry if your tulle doesn't match your cardstock exactly. The sheerness of the tulle allows it to blend well with colors in the same family.

instructions

1. Cut and fold bright yellow cardstock to make card.

2. Set eight eyelets; two on each corner of the card.

3. Cut four lengths of tulle and four pieces of gingham ribbon.

4. Run the ribbon through the eyelet and cross over two pieces of tulle as shown; tie in a knot. Do the same for the other three corners to make a frame around the outside of the card. Pink the edges of the tulle to uniform lengths.

5. Stamp the Queen image on a piece of bright pink cardstock using the black Memories ink and cut out. Pink the top and bottom and attach to the center of the card.

6. Computer journal your sentiment and print out on bright yellow cardstock. Cut out sentiment box and layer onto bright pink cardstock. Pink the edges of the pink cardstock.

7. Attach the sentiment box to the inside of the card. Set four Dotlets in the corners for added color.

Ribbon Petals Birthday

Jill Haglund

materials

Rubber Stamps: May Your Birthday be as Special as You Are by Hero Arts

Dye Inkpads: ColorBox Vivid (Pink) by Clearsnap

Papers: Lime Green Cardstock by Provo Craft; Hot Pink Paper: Local Craft Store

Buttons: Crazy Daisy Yellow Button by Favorite Findings

Ribbons: Local Craft Store

Adhesives: Terrifically Tacky Tape by Provo Craft; The Ultimate! Glue by Crafter's Pick; Foam Tape

Other: Hand-Cut Template (for the petals; see design); Waxed Paper

Tools: Non-Stick Scissors by Fiskars; Paper Cutter

tip! Tear the hot pink paper toward you so the white edge shows. Try inking the edges with a coordinating color.

instructions

1. Cut and fold lime green cardstock to make card.

2. Cut 7 petals from your petal template. Cover each petal with Terrifically Tacky Tape and trim excess tape.

3. Adhere different ribbon strips to cover the petals completely as shown. Trim each petal template to cut off any excess ribbon.

4. Glue down petals to card front.

5. Twist a piece of wide green polka-dotted ribbon for stem and tie a small piece to the center for leaves.

6. Place a small piece of waxed paper on top of card; add a book to dry overnight.

7. For inside, stamp birthday message in pink on yellow cardstock. Pink edges.

8. Tape to hot pink paper and tear to fit around message.

9. Add a strip of narrow ribbon to lime green paper and layer to wide green polka-dotted ribbon.

10. Attach sentiment piece with foam tape on top of ribbons.

11. Cut a strip of tulle 20" x 6". Wrap tulle around card and tie a knot at the top as shown. Cut another 2" x 4" piece and tie around the knot to make a flower; trim.

12. Add button to center of flower.

Enjoy Your Birthday

Nikki Cleary

materials

Rubber Stamps: Random Enjoy and Gift Montage by Stampendous; Enjoy Your Birthday by Hero Arts

Hybrid Inkpads: Palette Hybrid by Stewart Superior

Papers: White Textured Cardstock by DieCuts with a View; Numbers Black and White Patterned Paper by DieCuts with a View

Ribbons: May Arts and Doodlebug Design: Local Craft Store

Metal Items: Colored Staples by Making Memories

Adhesives: Glue Lines and Glue Dots by Glue Dots International

Other: Buttons; Flower Trim

Tools: Stapler; Paper Cutter by Fiskars; Pinking Shears by Mundial

instructions

1. Cut black cardstock into a 12" x 6" rectangle and fold in half.

2. Cut out a 5 ¾" square from white cardstock and adhere to front flap with Glue Dots.

3. Cut out a 5 ½" square from the patterned paper and adhere to front with Glue Dots.

4. Cut ribbons long enough to wrap around the front flap of card and adhere with Glue Lines. Attach button with Glue Dots. Run a small ribbon through the back of the button before tying it closed.

5. Stamp "Enjoy Your Birthday" on white cardstock and trim. Staple ribbons to stamped cardstock and adhere to front of card with Glue Dots.

6. Stamp Gift Montage on white cardstock and trim. Tear the bottom edge and adhere to the inside of card with Glue Dots.

7. Attach the flowers with Glue Lines.

8. Tie ribbon through the button and adhere with Glue Dot.

9. Stamp "Enjoy" on bottom of inside of card.

Happy Birthday Retro Floral

Amy Wellenstein

materials

Rubber Stamps: HAPPY and BIRTHDAY by Stampotique Originals; Small Round Tag by Paper Inspirations

Pigment Inkpads: VersaFine (Onyx Black) and VersaMark by Tsukineko

Papers: White, Black, Yellow and Pink Cardstock: Local Craft Store

Ribbons: Gingham Ribbon (Tangerine & Bumblebee) by Doodlebug Design: Local Craft Store

Buttons: Bubblegum Posies by Doodlebug Design

Adhesives: Foam Tape; Double-Stick Tape; The Ultimate! Glue by Crafter's Pick

Other: Waxed Linen Cord (Black)

instructions

1. Stamp circle repeatedly on a pink card using VersaMark ink.

2. Stamp "HAPPY BIRTHDAY"' on a strip of white cardstock. Layer onto black and yellow cardstock.

3. Adhere two narrow strips of black cardstock to the card. Use foam tape to attach the "HAPPY BIRTHDAY" panel to the card.

4. Adhere gingham ribbon to a strip of black cardstock and tape to card.

5. Tie waxed linen cord through the holes on a flower button and two tiny leaf buttons.

6. Glue the buttons to the ribbon strip.

tip! Stamp with VersaMark inkpads to allow your image to take on a slightly darker intensity of color than your paper. Perfect for backgrounds.

Floral Bouquet Birthday

Jill Haglund

materials

Rubber Stamps: Bouquet Montage by Stampendous

Dye Inkpads: ColorBox Vivid (Carnation) by Clearsnap

Papers: Floral and Stripes Paper from Mod by Autumn Leaves; Hot Pink and Turquoise Cardstock: Local Craft Store

Rub-Ons: Expressions Party Mix (White) by Doodlebug Design

Chipboard: Flower by Heidi Swapp

Metal Items: Large and Small Colored Brads by Making Memories

Ribbon: Local Craft Store

Adhesives: Scotch Double-Sided Sticky Tape by 3M; The Ultimate! Glue by Crafter's Pick

Tools: Paper Cutter; 1/8" Hand Punch

tip! For inside of card be sure you follow steps to ensure success; apply your rub-ons first! You may have to practice if you have never used them.

instructions

1. Cut and fold 12" x 6" hot pink cardstock for card. Cover card with striped paper.

2. Cut small 3" x 3" square and stamp floral image. Punch holes and add brads to center of flowers.

3. Layer stamped image onto floral paper to fit into pattern as shown.

4. Layer both onto striped paper and card front.

5. Glue 6" piece of ribbon to top and bottom of card.

6. For inside, cut turquoise piece of cardstock and apply happy birthday message and a small flower using Expressions rub-ons.

7. Cut and adhere a strip of ribbon for top of sentiment.

8. Punch hole in pink chipboard flower; add green brad and glue to ribbon on inside of card.

The cards in this section are festive enough to decorate with! Use them as centerpieces; make several different types and scatter them on a red-checkered tablecloth for your Fourth of July picnic. Make enlarged color copies for placemats; mat on red, white and blue colored paper. Or take them to a party as a hostess gift ... you are sure to earn plenty of stars (and stripes)!

Happy Fourth

Dawne Renee Pitts

materials

Rubber Stamps: Whispers Swoon Stretchy Star by Claudia Rose; Tall Alphabet by Stampotique Originals

Hybrid Inkpads: Palette Hybrid (Starry Night and L'Amour Red) by Stewart Superior

Papers: Card by Hero Arts; White Cardstock: Local Craft Store

Ribbons: Beaux Regards and Offray: Local Craft Store

Adhesives: Glue Lines by Glue Dots International; Art Accentz Terrifically Tacky Tape by Provo Craft

Other: White Buttons

Tools: Pinking Shears by Mundial; Sewing Machine

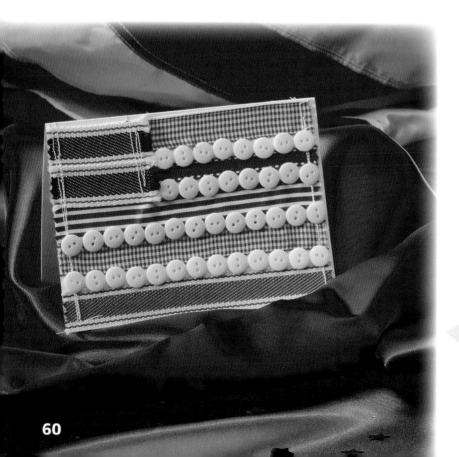

instructions

1. Cut and fold a piece of white cardstock to make card.

2. For front: Measure out your ribbons, leaving extra ribbon on each side. Allow space between each red ribbon for buttons. Tack down the ribbons in the middle of the page with adhesive to keep them in place while you sew.

3. Once tacked, use your sewing machine to carefully sew the edges of the ribbon. Trim off excess ribbon with pinking shears.

4. Use Glue Lines to attach the white buttons between the rows of red ribbons.

5. Adhere the sewn panel of cardstock to the card front with Art Accentz Terrifically Tacky Tape.

6. Stamp your sentiment on the inside of the card.

Fourth of July

Amy Wellenstein

materials

Rubber Stamps: Have a Star Spangled Day by Stampotique Originals; Star by Magenta; Firecracker by Whipper Snapper Designs

Pigment Inkpads: VersaFine (Satin Red and Onyx Black) by Tsukineko

Dye Inkpads: Memories (White) by Stewart Superior

Papers: White, Navy and Red Cardstock: Local Craft Store; Red Stripe by 7gypsies

Paints: Watercolors: Local Craft Store

Markers: Marvy Marker (Red) by Marvy Uchida

Tags: Holiday Metal-Rimmed Tags by K&Company

Ribbons: Red Satin, White Grosgrain and Navy Striped Ribbons by Offray; White Ribbon with Gold Stars: Local Fabric Store; Red and White Gingham Ribbon: Local Craft Store

Buttons: Gold and Blue Star by Streamline Buttons

Adhesives: Glue Stick; Xyron; Pop Up Glue Dots by Glue Dots International; Double-Stick Tape

Tools: Star Punch by Marvy Uchida

instructions

1. Stamp star repeatedly on a folded red card using white ink.

2. Adhere strips of ribbon at an angle to a panel of white cardstock using Xyron adhesive. Cut into two squares and adhere to the front of the card.

3. Stamp firecracker on a panel of white cardstock using Onyx Black ink. Color with watercolors and markers.

4. Layer the stamped panel on navy cardstock, then mount to the card using Glue Dots.

5. Thread red gingham ribbon through a metal-rimmed tag and tie into a bow. Secure to the card using a Glue Dot.

6. Use Glue Dots to secure coordinating buttons on the corners of the card.

7. Adhere a panel of striped paper to the inside of the card.

8. Stamp "Have a Star Spangled Day" on a strip of white cardstock using Red Satin ink. Punch a star out of one end.

9. Layer the sentiment on navy cardstock and adhere to the inside of the card.

Special Teacher

Kelly Lunceford

materials

Rubber Stamps: Alphabets and Fresh Fruits by Stampin' Up!

Pigment Inkpads: ColorBox (White) Brush Inkpad by Clearsnap

Dye Inkpads: Memories (Cherry Red) by Stewart Superior; Adirondack (Caramel) by Ranger Industries

Papers: Light Blue Cardstock by Bazzill Basics; Blue, Red, Yellow, Olive and Ivory Cardstock: Local Craft Store; Envelope Template by Martha by Mail

Computer Fonts: Book Antiqua (standard); Gutenberg by Creating Keepsakes

Ribbons: Red Gingham, Brown Grosgrain, Green Running Stripe: Local Craft Store

Adhesives: Glue Stick; Foam Tape

Tools: Paper Cutter; Stapler; Stylus

instructions

1. Cut a piece of blue cardstock 5" x 10". Fold in half to create a 5" x 5" card.

2. Attach a strip of olive cardstock as shown on card front.

3. Stamp apple image with red ink onto a rectangle of ivory cardstock. Stamp stem with Caramel ink and layer onto blue cardstock.

4. Stamp the "ABC's" with white ink onto a rectangle of red cardstock; frame matted apple image.

5. Cut a square of light blue cardstock and adhere to larger piece of yellow cardstock. Tie three ribbons around square in center. Attach to card with glue and staples.

6. Add entire apple image with foam to card front.

7. For inside of card: Print teacher quote in red onto a piece of ivory cardstock. Mat on a piece of red, then blue, then green, leaving enough space to add the author's name printed with brown ink. Add ribbon.

Envelope:

1. Trace envelope pattern onto a piece of red cardstock, add score marks with stylus and cut out. Assemble envelope with glue stick.

2. Stamp alphabet image onto the entire front side of the envelope with white ink. Let dry.

3. Tie a ribbon around envelope.

4. Stamp apple image again onto ivory cardstock and mat with blue. Attach to upper flap of envelope so that it can be opened.

A B C D E F G H I J K L M N O P

Chapter 11 · I Love My Teacher!

Every child has one — a favorite teacher who lingers in his or her memory long after the school year has come to a close. And teachers remember with fondness those long-ago classrooms and special students. Encourage your child to express their feelings while they are fresh! Go beyond "an apple for the teacher," a handmade card will be remembered forever. Get your son or daughter involved in this fulfilling family project; they will learn to express gratitude for their teacher's qualities and will see their efforts are much appreciated.

Happy New House

Amy Wellenstein

materials

Rubber Stamps: Classic Alphabet Set by Plaid;
2 Cuties Film by Catslife Press; Dots by Hot Potatoes

Pigment Inkpads: VersaFine (Onyx Black) and VersaMagic by Tsukineko

Papers: Teal and White Cardstock: Local Craft Store; Rainbow Sorbet from Lollipop Shoppe by Basic Grey; Green Tea Bitty Blossom by KI Memories

Ribbons: Bubblegum Rick Rack by Doodlebug Design: Local Craft Store

Adhesives: Double-Stick Tape; The Ultimate! Glue by Crafter's Pick; Glue Stick

Other: In Shapes Bloomers (Tropical) by Dress It Up Memory Mates by Jesse James & Co.

Tools: Sizzix Die Cutting Machine; Long Pentagon A Die by Provo Craft

instructions

1. Stamp a folded teal card with Dots using VersaMagic ink.

2. Die cut a small house from striped paper. Adhere to the card.

3. Stamp "HAPPY" along the bottom of the house.

4. Stamp one-half of 2 Cuties Film on white cardstock using Onyx Black ink. Adhere to the house.

5. Glue rick rack across the bottom of the card.

6. Glue small plastic flowers to the front of the card.

7. Stamp "NEW HOUSE" on green Tea Bitty Blossom paper using black ink. Adhere to the inside of the card.

Chapter 12 · New Home

When you trod over to the new neighbors' house with a basket of warm muffins, be sure to include a fun or sweet card to make them feel welcome! Who knows? You may even make a new friend who'll share with you the joy of stamping and card making. If you are moving and want to notify friends and family, make one special card, copy it, and just add ribbon!

HAPPY

New Home

Dawne Renee Pitts

materials

Rubber Stamps: Faux Post Cube by Just for Fun; Heart Pair by Paper Inspirations; Classic Uppercase and Lowercase Alphabet by Hero Arts

Dye Inkpads: Memories (Hunter Green) by Stewart Superior

Hybrid Inkpads: Palette Hybrid (Claret) by Stewart Superior

Papers: Purple Textured Gatefold Card by DieCuts with a View; Patterned Paper by Painted Purple from The Jenni Bowlin Collection by Li'l Davis Designs; White Cardstock: Local Craft Store

Rub-On Letters: Upper and Lower Case Rummage by Making Memories

Adhesive-Backed Items: Keyholes by Art Warehouse by Creative Imaginations

Ribbons: Pink Twill Cable by Art Warehouse by Creative Imaginations: Local Craft Store

Adhesives: Art Accentz Terrifically Tacky Tape by Provo Craft

Tools: Xacto Knife and Mat

instructions

1. Cut and tape two strips of the patterned paper to fit on the two "doors" of the card.

2. Adhere keyholes to card front and carefully cut out the middle of the locks with an xacto knife.

3. Using the rectangle and triangle of the Faux Postage Cube, stamp a house onto white cardstock using the Hunter Green ink.

4. Stamp the Heart Pair image inside the house using the Claret ink.

5. Cut out the house and adhere it to a strip of the patterned paper.

6. Use a mixture of the alphabet stamps and rub-ons to add your sentiment inside the card.

7. Tie the "doors" closed using the pink twill.

A girl party! How perfect! A shower is a fabulous reason for creating cards. Whether the occasion is a celebration of bride or baby, it's an opportunity to have a party before the real party begins! Encourage everyone involved to get together and discover how much fun they can have sharing ideas for making invitations, place cards, birth announcements or thank you cards.

Moon Belly

Nikki Cleary

materials

Rubber Stamps: Moon Belly by Stampotique Originals; Large Invitation by Rubber Stampede

Hybrid Inkpads: Palette Hybrid (Giverney Green and Claret) by Stewart Superior

Papers: Textured Cardstock by DieCuts With a View; Garden Party "Floral Friends" by Artic Frog

Ribbons: May Arts and Doodlebug Design: Local Craft Store

Metal Items: Colored Eyelets by Doodlebug Design

Adhesives: Glue Dots and Pop Up Glue Dots by Glue Dots International

Tools: Eyelet Setter and Hammer by Making Memories; Giga Merchandise Tag Punch by Marvy Uchida

Other: Makeup Sponge

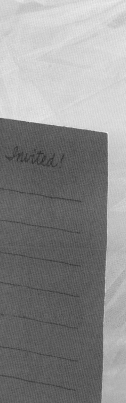

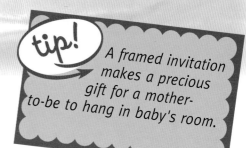

tip! *A framed invitation makes a precious gift for a mother-to-be to hang in baby's room.*

instructions

1. Cut cardstock and fold to make card desired size.
2. Cut patterned paper for front and adhere.
3. Set eyelets and tie on ribbon.
4. Adhere buttons in flower centers and rick rack.
5. Stamp "Moon Belly" on paper, cut to size and use a makeup sponge to add ink to edges, then adhere to card with Pop Up Glue Dots.
6. Stamp invitation on inside of card.
7. Punch out tag, set eyelet and tie with ribbon. Write the guest of honor's name and where she is registered.

Baby Blossom

Amy Wellenstein

instructions

1. Sand the edges of a square panel of polka dot paper.

2. Use double-stick tape to adhere a piece of green ribbon around the panel (tucking the ends on the back side).

3. Glue aqua and black rick rack to the panel (again hiding the ends on the back).

4. Adhere the panel to a folded turquoise card.

5. Stamp flower on a square of white cardstock using black ink; color with markers.

6. Layer the panel on turquoise cardstock, then affix to a square of black cardstock using foam tape.

7. Adhere the layered panel to the card using Glue Lines.

8. Trim off the prongs from the end of a rhinestone brad. Glue the rhinestone to an aqua button.

Moments Like This

Amy Wellenstein

materials

Rubber Stamps: Moments Like This by Danielle Johnson for Limited Edition Rubber Stamps

Dye Inkpads: Adirondack (Lettuce) by Ranger Industries

Papers: White, Teal, Pink and Orange Cardstock: Local Craft Store; Ice Cream Parlor (Simple Floral) by Pieces of Me by KI Memories; Pink Dot: Local Craft Store; Dumbo Stripe (Yellow) by Sandylion Sticker Designs; Sweet Potato Stripe by Bo Bunny Press; Spring Stripe by Pixie Press

Adhesives: Glue Stick; Double-Stick Tape; The Ultimate! Glue by Crafter's Pick

Other: Tiny Black Buttons; Clear Plexiglass Mount by Limited Edition Rubber Stamps

Tools: Flower Punches by EK Success

instructions

1. Affix the Moments Like This border stamp to a clear plexiglass mount (curving slightly to give the appearance of a stem).

2. Stamp on white cardstock using Lettuce ink. Repeat two more times at different angles.

3. Layer the white panel on teal cardstock and then on green floral paper. Mount these layers onto a folded white card.

4. Punch three large flowers and three small flowers from scraps of brightly colored papers.

5. Layer the flowers and adhere to the stems. Glue a tiny black button in the center of each flower.

6. Glue a strip of coordinating paper inside the card.

7. Stamp sentiment using Lettuce ink.

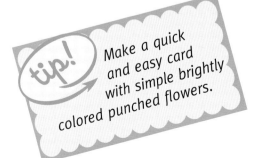

tip! Make a quick and easy card with simple brightly colored punched flowers.

Ava

Dawne Renee Pitts

materials

Rubber Stamps: Little Packages by Stampendous

Dye Inkpads: Memories (Black) by Stewart Superior

Pigment Inkpads: Palette Hybrid (Burnt Sienna) by Stewart Superior

Papers: Papers, Tag and File folder from the Lollipop Shoppe Collection by Basic Grey

Paint: Strawberries & Cream and Cranberry by Making Memories

Chipboard Alphabet: Schizophrenic Cotton Candy Alphabet by Heidi Swapp

Ribbons: Local Craft Store

Fabrics: Green Lace and Pink Tulle: Local Fabric Store

Adhesives: Art Accentz Terrifically Tacky Tape by Provo Craft; Designer Dries Clear Glue by Art Glitter

Tools: Sanding Block; Label Maker by Dymo; Aging Sponges by FoofaLa; Corner Rounder; Circle Punch by Marvy Uchida

instructions

1. Using the sanding block, sand the Basic Grey file folder.

2. Use the Strawberries & Cream paint with a small amount of the Cranberry paint. Apply two coats of paint to the chipboard letters and allow to dry.

3. Sand the chipboard letters to remove portions of the paint.

4. Use the FoofaLa aging sponge to apply Burnt Sienna ink to the chipboard letters; allow to dry and attach to front of file folder. The goal is to make them resemble the pink/red colors of the Basic Grey file folder.

5. Cut three coordinating pieces of Basic Grey paper and round the corners. Attach to inside of file folder, making sure they are even with the front of the file folder when closed.

6. Punch circles in the front and right side of file folder as shown.

7. Cut out baby's picture and position it so that it shows through the hole in the front of the file folder.

8. Cut a square from one of the Basic Grey solid papers and cut the square in half and at an angle to form a triangle. From the triangle, make photo corners. Attach to two corners of the picture.

9. Stamp the sentiment on a piece of the solid Basic Grey paper and attach. Sand the edges of the round Basic Grey tag and attach to the file folder.

10. Thread tag with lace and tulle and add lace to inside of card.

11. Use white label maker tape to emboss name and birthdate. Rub with Burnt Sienna ink and partially wipe off for a distressed look.

tip! Using photos in your cards makes them so much more personal!

Chapter 14 · New Baby

There is little in the world as precious as a new, velvety-soft, fresh-smelling baby. Once your little bundle arrives you'll want to share him or her with family and friends by sending an announcement. Peek at the next few pages for ideas to create your own original card to show just how special your new born really is!

Baby

Kelly Lunceford

B O Y

G I R L

materials

Rubber Stamps: I'm Here Stamp Set by Stampin' Up!

Dye Inkpads: Marvy Matchables (Blue) by Marvy Uchida; Embossing Powders (Light Blue): Local Craft Store

Papers: "Splash" Designer Series by Stampin' Up!; Yellow, White and Blue Cardstock: Local Craft Store

Ribbons: Blue Gingham: Local Craft Store

Buttons: Making Memories

Adhesives: Glue Stick; Mini Glue Dots by Glue Dots International; Scotch Tape by 3M

Other: Safety Pin

Tools: Paper Trimmer by Fiskars; Xacto Knife and Mat; 1/4-Inch Square Punch by Marvy Uchida; Heat Embossing Tool by Marvy Uchida; Tweezers

instructions

1. Cut a piece of 12" x 12" blue cardstock in half and fold to create a 6" x 6" card.

2. Cut a piece of designer paper slightly smaller than card front. Tape a strip of gingham ribbon to front of card, secure on back with tape.

3. Adhere square buttons to the top of the card with Glue Dots.

4. Stamp hand image onto white cardstock.

5. Cut a frame for the hand image from a square of yellow cardstock by measuring and cutting on a mat with an Xacto knife. Stamp alphabet over surface with blue ink.

6. Wrap gingham ribbon around right side of frame.

7. Use tweezers to hold safety pin and heat the tip with heat embossing tool. Dip the hot tip into the blue embossing powder with tweezers. Heat pin tip until embossing powder melts; pin through ribbon on frame.

8. Attach frame to a piece of blue cardstock with foam tape; hand image should be centered. Attach to card front.

9. Stamp alphabet onto yellow cardstock and punch out the letters to spell baby. Adhere to a piece of blue cardstock and attach to card.

Sailboat Baby Card

Kelly Lunceford

materials

Rubber Stamps:
Antique Alphabet
by PSX

Pigment Inkpads:
ColorBox (White) Cat's
Eye Inkpad by Clearsnap

Papers: Pink Collection
by Laura Ashley; Pink
and Green Cardstock
by Bazzill Basics; White
Cardstock: Local
Craft Store

Ribbon: Local Craft Store

Adhesives: Hermafix
Tabs; Mini Glue Dots by
Glue Dots International

Other: Button

Tools: Paper Trimmer by
Fiskars; Scallop Scissors
by Fiskars; Sewing
Machine

instructions

1. Cut pink cardstock 12" x 6" and score in half to create a 6" x 6" card.

2. Cut triangle shapes from two different patterned papers; trace a spool of ribbon to make a half-circle shape for boat base. Attach these shapes to the white cardstock to create the sailboat.

3. Cut a "flag" from pink ribbon and tuck under triangle sail with a bit of adhesive.

4. Sew around each piece for a quilted look.

5. Attach to the pink base and adhere button with a Mini Glue Dot.

6. Stamp the word "baby" with white pigment ink.

tip! Be sure to use the proper adhesive before running papers through a sewing machine. An adhesive that is too tacky may gum up your needle and ruin your machine.

Thank You Thank You

Nikki Cleary

materials

Rubber Stamps: Thank You by Stampendous; Thank You by Stampcraft

Hybrid Inkpads: Palette Hybrid (Giverney Green) by Stewart Superior

Papers: Orange Textured Cardstock by DieCuts with a View; Textured Paper by Fibermark; Pears with Script and Spring Caramel by Scenic Route; Wavy Ridge Bright Yellow Cardstock: Local Craft Store

Ribbons: May Arts and Making Memories: Local Craft Store

Adhesives: Xyron; Glue Dots and Glue Lines by Glue Dots International

Other: Buttons

Tools: Paper Cutter by Fiskars

instructions

1. Cut and fold cardstock to desired size to make card.

2. Cut Fibermark paper 1/4" smaller than front of card. Cut Pears with Script paper 1/4" smaller and adhere both papers with Xyron adhesive.

3. Cut two small squares of wavy ridge paper and Spring Caramel paper. Stamp "Thank You" on both squares of Spring Caramel paper.

4. Adhere ribbons to front of card and to the inside of card with Glue Dots and Glue Lines.

5. Cut tops of ribbons at various angles.

6. Adhere the wavy ridge and stamped paper to the front and inside of card with ribbons and buttons as shown.

7. Tie ribbons through buttons and adhere with Glue Dots to front of card.

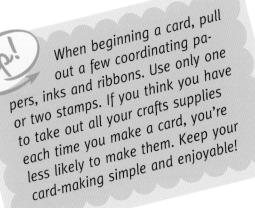

tip! When beginning a card, pull out a few coordinating papers, inks and ribbons. Use only one or two stamps. If you think you have to take out all your crafts supplies each time you make a card, you're less likely to make them. Keep your card-making simple and enjoyable!

Chapter 15 · Thank You, Miss You & Thinking of You

A handmade greeting is so much more than a card! Your time and effort demonstrates your heartfelt sentiments like nothing else can. Choose any theme, stamp or palette; let your imagination run wild. You can use the same designs for a thank you, miss you or thinking of you card. Take this opportunity to lift someone's spirits and brighten their day. Make them a card so they know you care!

Miss You

Dawne Renee Pitts

materials

Rubber Stamps: Row Faces Stamp by Stampotique Originals; Circle Pop Alphabet by Hero Arts; Antique Alphabet by PSX

Pigment Inkpads: ColorBox (Cyan) Pigment Brush Pad by Clearsnap

Hybrid Inkpads: Palette Hybrid (Burnt Sienna) by Stewart Superior

Papers: Gatefold Textured Card by DieCuts with a View; Patterned Paper from the Retro Stack by DieCuts with a View; White Cardstock: Local Craft Store

Metal Items: Dotlets by Doodlebug Design

Ribbons: SEI, May Arts and Offray: Local Craft Store

Adhesives: Art Accentz Terrifically Tacky Tape by Provo Craft

tip! Here's a good example of repeating a pattern in paper, stamps and letters.

instructions

1. Turn the gatefold card on its side. Cut a piece of patterned paper slightly smaller than the left side (the longer side) of the card.

2. Stamp the Row Faces on white cardstock and ink edges. Attach to the patterned paper with two Dotlets. Attach the patterned paper to the card front.

3. Cut a smaller piece of the patterned paper and attach to the right side of the card front (the smaller side).

4. Using the Circle Pop Alphabet stamps, stamp "W", "Y" and "G" with the ColorBox Cyan ink. Cut around the circle and ink the edges with Burnt Sienna ink.

5. Attach the circles to white cardstock and finish stamping the sentiment for the front of the card. Cut out the individual words into rectangles and ink the edges. Attach to the right front of the card.

6. Attach snips of coordinating ribbons to the inside of the card as shown. Using adhesive, close the entire right side of the card.

7. Stamp the inside sentiment onto rectangles of white cardstock; cut out and ink edges with Burnt Sienna ink. Attach to the left inside of the card.

8. Cut out circles from the patterned paper and attach around the inside sentiment.

Miss You

Nikki Cleary

materials

Rubber Stamps: Miss You and Friend by Rubber Stampede; Bouquet Montage by Stampendous

Hybrid Inkpads: Palette Hybrid (Orangerie) by Stewart Superior

Papers: Orange Textured Cardstock and Floral Prints by DieCuts with a View

Ribbons: May Arts, Offray and Doodlebug Design: Local Craft Store

Adhesives: Xyron; Glue Dots and Glue Lines by Glue Dots International

Tools: Paper Cutter by Fiskars

instructions

1. Cut yellow cardstock into a 5" x 12" rectangle and fold to make card. Cut the front flap shorter as shown.

2. Cut and layer orange cardstock and floral paper onto front of card as shown with Xyron adhesive.

3. Stamp "Miss You" on yellow cardstock and embellish with gold and white ribbon; layer onto orange cardstock. Use Xyron adhesive to layer piece to card front.

4. Add the ribbons to the inside front of card with Glue Lines.

5. Cut striped paper slightly smaller than inside of card and adhere.

6. Stamp Bouquet Montage on orange cardstock and adhere to inside of card.

7. Stamp "Friend" on yellow cardstock and layer onto blue ribbon and orange cardstock; attach to inside of card with Glue Dots.

8. Tie ribbon through button and adhere to inside of card.

Friend (frend) **n.1** a person whom one knows well and is fond of . 2. an ally, supporter, or sympathizer 3. loves you for who you are. 4. unconditionally accepts you.

instructions

1. Cut and fold bright yellow cardstock.
2. Cut and glue patterned papers to card front with Xyron adhesive.
3. Glue strips of cut ribbons on each side of card using Xyron adhesive or glue stick.
4. Add green frame with Glue Dots.
5. Cut small rectangle from pink paper and stamp "Miss you" in lime green ink, add to inside of frame with Glue Dots.
6. Layer pink rick rack over ribbon.
7. Tie a green ribbon and attach with Glue Dots.
8. Adhere vintage button and stacked buttons to front of card using Glue Dots.
9. Open card and use glue stick or Xyron adhesive to glue down ribbons and rick rack as shown.
10. Use Glue Dots to add buttons.
11. Stamp Love Wire image in Orchid ink.

Miss You

Lindsay Haglund

materials

Rubber Stamps: Circle Pop Alphabet by Hero Arts; Love Wire by Stampendous

Pigment Inkpads: ColorBox (Orchid and Moss Green) Cat's Eye by Clearsnap

Papers: Patterned Paper by SEI; Bright Yellow and Pink Cardstock: Local Craft Store

Metal Items: Frame Kit (Lime Green Frame) by Heidi Swapp

Ribbons: May Arts and Beaux Regards; Rick Rack by Doodlebug Design: Local Craft Store

Adhesives: Xyron; Glue Dots by Glue Dots International; Glue Stick

Other: Vintage Button; Other Buttons

Tools: Paper Cutter

 tip! Keep your eye out for vintage buttons. They can become the focus of a beautifully designed card.

Get Well Soon

Nikki Cleary

materials

Rubber Stamps: Friendly Messages "thinking of you" by Stampendous; Get Well Soon from Rubber Stampede by Delta

Dye Inkpads: Ancient Page (Chocolate) by Clearsnap

Papers: Brown and Green Textured Cardstock and Floral and Square Retro Prints by DieCuts With a View

Metal Items: Green Colored Staples by Making Memories

Ribbons: May Arts, Li'l Davis Designs and Local Craft Store

Adhesives: Scotch Double-Sided Sticky Tape by 3M; Glue Dots by Glue Dots International

Other: Buttons

Tools: Paper Cutter by Fiskers; Scissors and Pinking Shears by Mundial; Stapler

instructions

1. Cut blue cardstock 4" x 8" and fold in half to make card.

2. Cut green cardstock into 3 3/4" squares; adhere to front of card.

3. Layer 3 1/2" square of retro floral print paper to green cardstock.

4. Wrap two widths of ribbons around front flap of card and adhere to front and back with Glue Dots.

5. Stamp "thinking of you" on blue cardstock, trim and snip end with pinking shears, Layer onto a piece of brown textured paper and use Glue Dots to attach to card.

6. Cut 2" snippet of blue ribbon and sandwich between buttons in button stack; adhere to front of card with Glue Dots.

7. To finish inside, cut 3 3/4" square of brown paper and layer 3 1/2" square retro print.

8. Stamp "Get Well Soon" on green cardstock and trim. Layer onto blue cardstock, trim and cut bottom with pinking shears.

9. Staple 2" piece of ribbon to the sentiment with colored staple. Attach to card with Glue Dots.

10. Adhere the three buttons with Glue Dots as shown.

Thinking of You Always Makes Me Smile

Amy Wellenstein

materials

Rubber Stamps: Boy by Stampotique Originals; Magnetic Alphabet (Providence) by Making Memories

Dye Inkpads: Impress (Pansy) and VersaFine (Onyx Black) by Tsukineko

Papers: White, Lime Green and Turquoise Cardstock: Local Craft Store

Ribbons: Local Craft Store

Buttons: Hand-Dyed Buttons (Bright Assortment) by Doodlebug Design

Adhesives: Double-Stick Tape

Other: Embroidery Floss (White)

instructions

1. Stamp boy on a lime green panel using Pansy ink.

2. Stamp "Thinking of you always makes me smile" on white cardstock using Onyx Black ink. Cut the words apart and adhere the "Thinking of you" to the lime green panel.

3. Use double-stick tape to adhere a piece of ribbon around the right-hand side of the card.

4. Layer the stamped panel on white cardstock.

5. Sew coordinating buttons to the upper left corner using embroidery floss.

6. Mount the embellished panel on a folded turquoise card.

7. Adhere the "always makes me smile" to the inside of the card.

8. Wrap another piece of the same ribbon around a strip of lime green cardstock and adhere to the lower edge of the inside of the card.

Thank You Friend

Amy Wellenstein

materials

Rubber Stamps: Thank You and Friend by Stampotique Originals

Pigment Inkpads: VersaFine (Onyx Black) by Tsukineko

Papers: Purple, Green, White and Turquoise Cardstock: Local Craft Store; Green Tea Bitty Blossom by KI Memories; Dotted Lines (Seabreeze) by Doodlebug Design

Transparencies: Clear Transparency: Local Office Supply

Ribbons: Purple Ribbon by May Arts: Local Craft Store

Sequins: Flower Sequins (Seabreeze) by Doodlebug Design

Adhesives: Glue Stick; Foam Tape; Double-Stick Tape

Tools: Small, Large and Medium Circle Punches by Marvy Uchida

instructions

1. Adhere green floral paper to the front of a folded green card.

2. Use a small circle punch to punch a hole near the bottom on the front of the card.

3. Punch a large circle from purple cardstock. Punch a small offset circle out of the larger circle.

4. Line the purple circle and the opening in the front of the card with clear transparency.

5. Pile several flower sequins on the face of the card (centering them in the window) and attach the purple circle using foam tape. These layers will create a "shaker box."

6. Stamp "Thank You" on a strip of white cardstock using Onyx Black ink. Layer on turquoise cardstock.

7. Use double-stick tape to secure a piece of purple ribbon around the front of the card.

8. Use foam tape to adhere the "Thank You" panel over the ribbon.

9. Adhere a strip of coordinating paper to the inside of the card.

10. Stamp "Friend" in the lower right corner.

11 Punch a medium circle from striped paper. Glue inside the card behind the window.

tip! Dress up your cards with sequins! Find them for all occasions in any party store.

discoveR the
miRacle
iN each
new daY

INSPIRATION

es · happine
), bless·ing
< bletsian ·

[grat·i·tude]

thinking of you

Blessing

Lindsay Haglund

materials

Papers: Purple Diamond-Patterned Card by Making Memories; White, Light Green, Blue and Pink Textured Papers by Canson

Adhesive-Backed Words and Images: Pink Butterflies by K&Company

Epoxy Stickers: Discover the Miracle in Each New Day and INSPIRATION by Danielle Johnson for Creative Imaginations; Transparent Epoxy Sticker (Blessing) by Karen Russell for Creative Imaginations

Ribbons: Local Craft Store

Adhesives: Glue Stick; Glue Dots by Glue Dots International

instructions

1. Cut a square of green paper and a rectangle of blue paper; adhere to card with glue stick.

2. Adhere all ribbons to card with glue stick.

3. Back the "Blessing" definition with white paper and trim.

4. Back the word "INSPIRATION" with light pink paper and trim.

5. Back "discover the miracle in each new day" with light green paper and trim.

6. Adhere all pieces onto card front as shown.

7. Press adhesive-backed butterflies to card.

8. Tie green ribbon in a knot and add to bottom left of card front with Glue Dot.

Gratitude

Lindsay Haglund

materials

Papers: Patterned Papers by SEI; Scalloped Pre-Made Card from Making Memories; Cardstock: Local Craft Store

Epoxy Sticker: Creative Imaginations

Ribbons: Local Craft Store

Adhesives: Glue Dots by Glue Dots International; Art Accentz Terrifically Tacky Tape by Provo Craft; Foam Tape

Tools: Pinking Shears by Mundial

instructions

1. Cut scalloped edge on patterned paper to match scallop edge on card; tape to top of card.

2. Cut striped paper and cardstock to fit card front and tape as shown.

3. Wrap ribbon around the card; meet bends on the back of card and tape together.

4. Stamp sentiment on cardstock, pink edges and attach to front with foam tape.

5. On the back of card, tuck narrow ribbon under wide polka-dotted ribbon. Bring around to the front of card and slip under striped paper for closure.

6. Tie bow with narrow ribbon and use Glue Dots to attach to flap.

7. Press epoxy Gratitude sticker to front of card.

tip! Epoxy stickers backed with light-colored paper give the appearance of "stamped images."

Love
Dianne Frailing

materials

Rubber Stamps: Love Wire by Paper Inspirations; Reverse Collage Heart by Paper Inspirations

Dye InkPads: Tim Holtz (Fired Brick) Distress Ink by Ranger Industries

Papers: Raspberry Textured Cardstock by Doodlebug Design and Fibermark; Square Garden by Artic Frog

Ribbons: May Arts: Local Craft Store

Buttons: Shabby Chick by Doodlebug Design

Adhesives: Glue Dots by Glue Dots International; Glue Stick

Tools: Sewing Machine; Pinking Shears by Mundial; Paper Cutter by Fiskars

instructions

1. Cut raspberry cardstock to 5" x 11" and fold in half to make card.

2. Cut green textured paper into a 5 1/4" square, then cut diagonally to make a triangle.

3. Sew triangle to top of card continuing around four sides of card front using medium width zigzag stitch.

4. Choose three or four coordinating ribbons and stitch or glue onto large triangle.

5. Stamp a large heart on top of the card opposite the large triangle.

6. Cut one or more ribbons for the loop to open card. Sew loop to card. Secure the raw edge of loop to the card with a button.

7. Make a large bow with wide ribbon and tie bow at center with a coordinating narrow ribbon.

8. Adhere ribbon to inside of card as shown.

9. Cut coordinating rectangle of Square Garden paper with pinking shears slightly smaller than inside of card; adhere with glue stick.

10. Stamp the inside of the card with Love Wire image.

tip! Use a snippet of ribbon tied onto your bow to hold it in place and to add color to your card. Pink scrapbook paper and glue inside for your handwritten message.

Thinking of You at the Cafe

Jill Haglund

materials

Rubber Stamp: Rubber Stampede by Delta

Dye Inkpads: ColorBox Vivid (Turquoise) by Clearsnap

Papers: Hot Pink, Turquoise, Deep Red and Light Pink Cardstock by DieCuts with a View; Chester Collection by me & my BIG ideas

Rub-Ons: Expressions (Hot Pink and Lime Green) by Doodlebug Design

Metal Items: Pink Square Brads by Making Memories

Ribbons: Local Craft Store

Adhesives: Scotch Double-Sided Sticky Tape by 3M; The Ultimate! Glue by Crafter's Pick

Other: Pink Button Thread; Button

Tools: Paper Cutter; Hand Punch

tip! Brads are always a nice finishing touch to any card!

instructions

1. Cut and fold hot pink cardstock.
2. Layer entire card with Chester Collection printed floral paper.
3. Cut and layer four solid colors of cardstock as shown. Punch all four corners and add pink square brads for decoration.
4. Stamp image in turquoise ink and tape to panel. Adhere panel to front of card with tape.
5. Trim out card with ribbon on all four sides using The Ultimate! Glue.
6. For inside, apply rub-ons to spell "Thinking of you" onto white cardstock.
7. Cut into a rectangle and layer to a piece of turquoise cardstock.
8. Add a snippet of ribbon and button.

Best Witches

Dawne Renee Pitts

materials

Rubber Stamps: "Whoosh" by PSX; Bella Geste Alphabet Set by Hampton Art

Dye Inkpads: Memories (Black) by Stewart Superior

Papers: Purple, Yellow and Orange Cardstock: Local Craft Store

Metal Items: Orange Brads: Local Craft Store

Ribbons: May Arts: Local Craft Store

Adhesives: Pop Up Glue Dots by Glue Dots International; Art Accentz Terrifically Tacky Tape by Provo Craft

Tools: Pinking Shears by Mundial

Chapter 16 · Halloween

Aren't these little witches adorable? Too cute to be scary! Dig out papers and ribbons in oranges, purples, greens, yellows and blacks and have a card making frenzy! These are thoughtful non-candy treats for your kids, nephews and nieces or the special little tykes in your neighborhood. When they come 'round, asking "trick or treat?" you'll be ready with treasures they'll hold dear for years.

instructions

1. Cut and fold purple cardstock to make card.

2. Stamp "Whoosh" on yellow cardstock using black ink. Cut out as shown, angling one end.

3. Cut out a slightly larger piece of orange cardstock, angling one side. Use tape to layer the yellow cardstock over the orange piece.

4. Attach snips of the green and yellow ribbon to each corner of the yellow cardstock using the orange brads. Pink ribbon ends after placement.

5. Attach panel to the front of the card using Pop Up Glue Dots.

6. Stamp your inside sentiment on yellow cardstock, pink one edge and adhere to inside of card.

Natalie

Dawne Renee Pitts

materials

Rubber Stamps: Natalie by Rubber Moon; Mara Mi Alphabet Stamps by Hampton Art

Dye Inkpads: Memories (Black) by Stewart Superior

Papers: Orange and Black Cardstock

Metal Items: Black Eyelets and Black and Orange Dotlets by Doodlebug Design

Ribbons: Gingham Ribbon by Close to My Heart; Orange and White Gingham by Offray: Local Craft Store

Adhesives: Art Accentz Terrifically Tacky Tape by Provo Craft

tip! Jazz up any card with a coordinating ribbon frame.

instructions

1. Make a card body using orange cardstock.

2. Stamp Natalie image on orange cardstock.

3. Set two black eyelets in each corner of the orange cardstock.

4. Thread black and white gingham ribbon through the eyelets and tie in double knots.

5. Mount orange cardstock onto black cardstock.

6. Make a frame around the orange cardstock using orange and white gingham ribbon secured with black Dotlets.

7. Mount the orange and black cardstocks onto the orange card body.

8. For the inside of the card, pink edges of black cardstock and attach orange Dotlets.

9. Stamp "Boo" message onto a small piece of orange cardstock using black ink.

10. Attach the piece of orange cardstock to the black piece of cardstock on the inside of the card.

Chapter 17 · Thanksgiving

This joyful card incorporates clever little ideas; Amy Wellenstein used a small handprint for a turkey's body and inks in autumn colors to create a greeting anyone would welcome in their mailbox. Thanksgiving is a time to be grateful for your blessings. Express your gratitude with this card; your efforts will be appreciated more than you know.

Happy Turkey Day

Amy Wellenstein

materials

Rubber Stamps: Handprint by PSX; Alphabet Set by Rusty Pickle; Bird Image by Catslife Press

Pigment Inkpads: VersaFine (Onyx Black) by Tsukineko

Hybrid Inkpads: Palette Hybrid (Landscape) by Stewart Superior

Papers: White, Brown, Green, Orange and Yellow Cardstock: Local Craft Store; Harvest Stripes by Frances Meyer

Ribbons: May Arts: Local Craft Store

Buttons: Large Green Buttons by Doodlebug Design; Yellow Buttons: Local Craft Store

Adhesives: Foam Tape; Double-Stick Tape; Glue Stick; The Ultimate! Glue by Crafter's Pick; Pop-Up Glue Dots by Glue Dots International

Other: Chipboard

tip! From handprint to turkey - a delightful example of multiple image use!

instructions

1. Stamp handprint on white cardstock using Landscape ink.

2. Ink only the legs of a bird image with Onyx Black ink and stamp at the bottom of the handprint.

3. Use orange cardstock to make a tiny beak. Adhere to the stamped image.

4. Layer the stamped panel on brown cardstock.

5. Adhere orange striped paper to chipboard for stability. Wrap with green ribbon, securing ends on the back side with double-stick tape.

6. Use Glue Dots to adhere the stamped panel to the striped panel.

7. Layer on green cardstock, then mount on a folded yellow card.

8. Glue coordinating buttons to the front of the card.

9. Stamp "Happy Turkey Day" on white cardstock using Landscape ink.

10. Cut the words apart, layer on striped paper, and adhere to the inside of the card.

Christmas Wishes

Dawne Renee Pitts

tip! A simple stamped Christmas sentiment is all you need for the inside

tip! Use some of the same papers to make an envelope to match your card.

instructions

1. Cut and score red cardstock for 6" x 6" card.

2. Cut a piece of the Making Memories Lime Dots paper slightly smaller than 6" x 6" and round the corners with the corner rounder. Ink the edges of the page using the ColorBox Charcoal ink (the Cat's Eye pads work best for this). Adhere this piece of lime paper to the front of the red card and set aside.

3. Cut a piece of red cardstock approximately 5 1/2" x 5 1/2" and round the corners with the corner rounder. Cut a piece of Dreamy Dots paper and round the corners.

4. Use the circle punch to punch out 45 circles from the Making Memories Lime Dots paper. Ink the edges of each circle with ColorBox Charcoal ink.

5. To make the Christmas tree, adhere the green circles to the 5" x 5" piece of red cardstock, beginning on the bottom row with 9 circles; the next row will be 8, then 7, 6, 5, 4, 3, 2 and 1. Overlap the circles where necessary to cover up all red spaces.

6. Cut a small piece of brown rick rack for the trunk of the tree and adhere to the card.

7. Layer red cardstock over green Dreamy Dots and adhere to card front.

8. Use selected stamps from Christmas Dots Collection to stamp words. Cut out and add to tree with foam tape.

Chapter 18 · Christmas

Once you have felt the spirit of Christmas and finished decorating the house, pull out all the red and green papers, ribbons, buttons and tulle. Listen to Christmas music, roll up your sleeves, and instead of -- or in addition to -- making Christmas cookies, make Christmas cards! Invite a friend or neighbor to make the experience more meaningful. There are endless Christmas images and messages available; choose several favorites and make six to a dozen of each.

Ho Ho Ho

Dawne Renee Pitts

materials

Rubber Stamps: Retro Santa by PSX; Ho Ho Ho by Rubber Stampede

Dye Inkpads: Memories (Black) by Stewart Superior

Papers: Green Cardstock: Local Craft Store

Tag: American Tag Company or Local Craft Store

Metal Items: Eyelets by Doodlebug Design or Local Craft Store

Ribbons: Red and Green Gingham by Offray: Local Craft Store

Adhesives: Art Accentz Terrifically Tacky Tape by Provo Craft

instructions

1. Cut and fold green cardstock to make card.

2. Stamp Santa image on white cardstock with black ink. Cut out as shown.

3. Set two green eyelets in the top two corners of the white cardstock.

4. Set red and green eyelets across the bottom of the white cardstock.

5. Tie green and red gingham ribbon through the eyelets.

6. Mount the stamped and embellished white cardstock on the front of the card.

7. Stamp "ho ho ho" on the white tag.

8. Set a green eyelet in the tag.

9. Tie a piece of red gingham through the tag.

10. Mount the tag on the inside of the card.

Merry Little Christmas

Amy Wellenstein

Rubber Stamps: Dog and Christmas Tree by Stampotique Originals; Have Yourself a Merry Little Christmas by Dawn Houser for Inkadinkado Rubber Stamps

Pigment Inkpads: VersaFine (Onyx Black) by Tsukineko

Dye Inkpads: Archival Ink (Maroon) by Ranger Industries

Papers: White, Red, Hunter and Pink Cardstock: Local Craft Store; Green Tea Bitty Blossom and Petite Pop by KI Memories

Colored Pencils: Prismacolor (Yellow, Red and Brown) by Stanford

Ribbons: Pink Ribbon with Red Edges by May Arts; Sheer Burgundy Ribbon: Local Craft Store

Adhesives: Foam Tape; Double-Stick Tape; Mini Glue Dots by Glue Dots International; The Ultimate! Glue by Crafter's Pick; Glue Stick

Other: Buttons

instructions

1. Cut and fold red cardstock to make card.

2. Layer green floral patterned paper on pink cardstock. Cut a slit in either end and insert a piece of ribbon. Use double-stick tape to adhere the ends of the ribbon to the backside of the panel. Adhere panel to card.

3. Stamp Dog on white cardstock using Onyx Black ink. Color with colored pencils.

4. Layer the stamped panel on hunter green and red cardstocks, then adhere to the front of the card using foam tape.

5. Further embellish the front of the card with a sheer ribbon bow and coordinating buttons.

6. Stamp Christmas Tree on a panel of green floral paper using maroon ink.

7. Stamp phrase next to the tree using Onyx Black ink. Adhere to the inside of the card.

Colorful Christmas

Dawne Renee Pitts

materials

Rubber Stamps: Ready for Christmas Stamp by PSX; Good Alphabet by Hero Arts

Dye Inkpads: Memories (Black) by Stewart Superior

Hybrid Inkpads: Palette Hybrid (Iris) by Stewart Superior

Papers: Pink Cardstock: Local Craft Store; Textured Cardstock by Bazzill (Doodlebug Limeade Green) and DieCuts with a View (Salmon)

Rub-On Letters: Doodlebug Design and Making Memories

Metal Items: Dotlets and Eyelets by Doodlebug Design

Ribbons: All Gingham by Nice & Narrow by Offray: Local Craft Store

Adhesives: Art Accentz Terrifically Tacky Tape by Provo Craft

Other: Star Gem

Tools: Scallop Paper Edgers by Fiskars; Fantastix Coloring Tool Brush Point by Tsukineko

tip! Try altering your design by adding buttons, brads, ribbons and glitter to the stamped image.

instructions

1. Cut and fold a card from salmon textured cardstock.

2. Stamp Ready for Christmas image on pink cardstock. Add Dotlets in the ornaments and glue a sparkly star on top of the "hair" on the stamped Christmas tree image.

3. Use the Tsukineko Fantastix Coloring Tool Brush and Iris inkpad to color in the present.

4. Use the scallop scissors to cut the top and bottom of the stamped image on pink cardstock.

5. Cut a piece of Bazzill Doodlebug Limeade textured cardstock.

6. Set eyelets down either side of the front of the card, using various bright colors.

7. Run ribbon through the eyelets, tying them in various knots and wrapping around the corners of the card.

8. Adhere the Limeade cardstock strip at an angle between the rows of eyelets.

9. Attach the pink cardstock with the Christmas image at an angle to the Limeade cardstock.

10. Using a Making Memories rub-on, place the word "Joy" on the bottom of the Limeade cardstock strip.

11. Using various colors of the Doodlebug rub-ons, Making Memories rub-ons and Hero Arts stamps, create your inside sentiment on a square of pink cardstock. Adhere to the inside of the card.

12. Cut a square of the Limeade cardstock, then cut the square in half on an angle to make two photo corners; adhere them to two corners of the message inside the card.

Happy Holidays with Tree Card

Amy Wellenstein

materials

Rubber Stamps: Christmas Tree, Happy and Holidays by Stampotique Originals

Pigment Inkpads: VersaFine (Satin Red) by Tsukineko

Papers: Green and White Cardstock: Local Craft Store; Red Hot Solid, Envy Mini Bangles, and Petite Pop by KI Memories

Tags: Holiday Metal-Rimmed Tags by K&Company

Ribbons: Assorted Ribbons: Local Craft Store

Adhesives: Glue Stick, Xyron, Pop Up Glue Dots by Glue Dots International; The Ultimate! Glue by Crafter's Pick; Double-Stick Tape

Other: Buttons

Tools: Circle Punch by Marvy Uchida

tip! Repeat a pattern throughout your card, such as dots or circles, with circle punches, round buttons and patterned paper.

instructions

1. Adhere strips of ribbon to a panel of white cardstock using Xyron adhesive.

2. Adhere green and polka dot patterned papers to a folded red card.

3. Adhere the ribbon panel to the card.

4. Stamp Christmas Tree on white cardstock using Red Satin ink. Layer on a green panel and adhere to the card using Glue Dots.

5. Thread white ribbon through a metal-rimmed tag and tie into a bow; secure to the card using a Glue Dot.

6. Glue coordinating buttons down one edge of the ribbon panel.

7. Punch three circles from dark green cardstock and adhere to the right edge of the card.

8. Embellish the inside of the card with a stamped sentiment, coordinating patterned papers and another green cardstock circle.

Christmas
memories

Merry Christmas

Jill Haglund

materials

Rubber Stamps: Merry Christmas with Santa and Merry & Bright from Retro Holiday Set from Rubber Stampede by Delta; Ho Ho Ho by Inkadinkado Rubber Stamps

Markers: Red and Green by Marvy

Papers: White, Red and Green Cardstock: Local Craft Store; Green, White and Red Striped Paper by K&Company

Tags: Local Craft Store or Office Supply

Ribbons: Local Craft Store

Adhesives: Scotch Double-Sided Sticky Tape by 3M; The Ultimate! Glue by Crafter's Pick

Other: Small Buttons

Tools: Hand Punch; Paper Cutter

instructions

1. Cut and fold red cardstock to make card.

2. Cut all other papers as shown.

3. Color Santa image using a red marker and Merry Christmas using green marker; stamp on white cardstock.

4. Use a green marker to color and stamp Ho on three tags; use red marker to ink edges of tags. Remove the string in the tags and replace with short ribbon piece.

5. Flip over Santa image and tape all three stamped tags to back of card.

6. Layer image onto all other papers; tape to card front.

7. Place a dab of The Ultimate! Glue onto three buttons and place where ribbon meets white cardstock.

8. For the inside, stamp Merry and Bright on white cardstock using the green and red markers again; edge the cardstock with red marker. Punch a hole in the top center and thread with ribbon snippet. Make a small ribbon bow to match.

9. Layer to a rectangle of the striped paper; glue on tips of ribbon snippet and the small bow as shown.

Happy Holidays

Jill Haglund

materials

Rubber Stamps: Santa by All Night Media/Plaid; Happy Holidays: Local Craft Store

Pigment Inkpads: ColorBox (White) by Clearsnap

Dye Inkpads: ColorBox Vivid (Red) by Clearsnap

Embossing Powders: White: Local Craft Store

Papers: White, Red and Green Cardstock

Metal Items: Green Brads

by Making Memories

Buttons: White and Snowflake Buttons by Fancy Findings

Ribbons: Local Craft Store

Adhesives: Scotch Double-Sided Sticky Tape by 3M; Glue Dots by Glue Dots International

Tools: Paper Cutter by Fiskars; Pinking Shears by Mundial; 1/2" Punch, 2" Super Punch, Round Punch and Embossing Heat Tool by Marvy Uchida

instructions

1. Cut and fold red cardstock to make card.

2. Cut a 5" x 3 1/2" piece of green paper. Stamp snowflake pattern to cover paper in white ink.

3. Sprinkle embossing powder onto paper, then shake excess off onto scrap paper; pour excess back into embossing powder container and replace cap to reuse. Use heat tool to emboss snowflakes, making sure the image is totally embossed.

4. Cut a 6" x 6" piece of red paper. Stamp snowflakes and Santa in white and emboss, following instructions above.

5. Flip over the punch and insert green snowflake patterned paper; line up paper and punch a half-round shape in top center.

6. Fold on sides as shown and tape back to make a pocket. Tie on a 7" piece of ribbon and pink the ends. Add pocket to card front.

7. Punch out white embossed snowflakes and apply to card with Glue Dots.

8. Cut a 3/4" wide strip of green paper to fit onto length of your card. Glue ribbon to paper strip. Glue buttons to ribbon.

9. For tag, cut and layer white red and green cardstock. Pink top of white cardstock.

10. Punch hole in top and add a 2 1/2" snippet of ribbon with a green brad.

11. Stamp Santa in red ink onto white cardstock. Emboss Santa using white embossing powder on red cardstock.

12. Cut out Santa stamped in red. Cut out hat from the white embossed image. Glue Red hat to Santa as shown. Glue entire Santa to tag.

13. For inside, stamp "Happy Holidays" in red on white cardstock and pink one end. Layer onto green cardstock and punch hole. Add 2 1/2" ribbon snippet with a green brad.

Feliz Navidad

Jill Haglund

materials

Rubber Stamps: Feliz Navidad with Christmas Bulbs by All Night Media/Plaid

Pigment Inkpads: ColorBox Brush (Green) by Clearsnap

Papers: Green and White Cardstock: Local Craft Store; Vellum Glittering Snowflakes by K&Company

Green Metal Brads: Making Memories

Ribbons: Various Green and Red Ribbons: Local Craft Store

Adhesives: Scotch Double-Sided Sticky Tape by 3M; The Ultimate! Glue by Crafter's Pick

Other: Waxed Paper

Tools: Pinking Shears; Paper Cutter; Hand Punch

tip! Make sure to glue on the ribbons last, cover ribbon area with waxed paper and press with a heavy book to dry overnight.

instructions

1. Cut and fold green cardstock to make card; set aside.

2. Cut and layer papers as shown to make a panel.

3. Stamp "Feliz Navidad" in green on white cardstock, pink edges and tape to panel.

4. Punch holes as shown, insert brads and open backs to secure.

5. Tape the entire panel onto the green card.

6. Cut a piece of ribbon 2" wider then card; tie short snippets every 3/4" to the long piece of ribbon. Pink all ribbon ends.

7. Glue ribbon piece to top of card with The Ultimate! Glue.

8. Adjust ribbon position as desired and allow glue to dry.

Joy to the World

Jill Haglund

materials

Rubber Stamps: Christmas Ornaments from the Retro Holiday Set from Rubber Stampede by Delta

Dye Inkpads: ColorBox Vivid (Green and Red) by Clearsnap

Papers: Green, Dark Red and White Cardstock: Local Craft Store

Metal Items: Ribbon Charms by Scrapworks; Metal Alphadotz: Local Craft Store

Ribbons: Local Craft Store

Adhesives: Scotch Double-Sided Sticky Tape by 3M; The Ultimate! Glue by Crafter's Pick

Tools: Paper Cutter

tip! Be sure to cut your ribbon at a sharp angle before beginning to thread the ribbon charms. You may have to do this more than once when threading several charms.

instructions

1. Cut and fold cardstock to make card.

2. Stamp ornaments in red and green as shown. Cut out and layer onto green cardstock and trim.

3. Tape ornaments onto card.

4. Cut ribbon to "hang" ornaments and make small bows. Make your bows as small as possible and tie them tightly before snipping ends.

5. Add ribbon and bows to ornament with glue.

6. Thread and center "JOY" onto ribbon and glue to card.

7. For inside, thread "TO THE WORLD" onto ribbon and glue to inside, trimming ends.

It's Cold Outside

Jill Haglund

tip! Tags threaded with ribbon snippets are a delightful way to add small sentiments or images to the inside of a card.

materials

Rubber Stamps: Snowman, Baby It's Cold Outside, Mittens and Warm Wishes by All Night Media/Plaid; Retro Snowflake by Hot Potatoes

Pigment Inkpads: ColorBox Brush (Blue) by Clearsnap

Dye Inkpads: Adirondack Stonewashed by Ranger Industries

Embossing Powders: White: Local Craft Store

Papers: White and Blue Cardstock: Local Craft Store

Tags: Small Round Metal-Rimmed Tags: Local Craft Store or Office Supply

Buttons: Snowflake Buttons: Local Craft Store

Ribbons: Blue Ribbons: Local Craft Store

Adhesives: Scotch Double-Sided Sticky Tape by 3M; Glue Dots by Glue Dots International

Tools: Paper Cutter by Fiskars, Shank cutter

instructions

1. Cut and fold white cardstock to make card or use pre-made card.

2. Stamp Retro Snowflake in Stonewashed ink for background.

3. Stamp Snowman in ColorBox Blue ink, trim. Cut papers and layer Snowman on top.

4. Trim out design with blue ribbon mitered at corners and glued to card.

5. Cut shanks off snowflake buttons. Adhere with Glue Dots in all four corners of card design as shown.

6. For inside, cut two blue panels as shown. Trim all corners with one 1 1/2" piece of ribbon glued to front. Trim, fold and tape to secure ribbon to back of panel.

7. Stamp messages on round tags in Memories Blue ink and tie a snippet of ribbon through each one. Add to card with Glue Dots.

Hippest of Cats

Amy Wellenstein

materials

Rubber Stamps: Big Sprinkle and Little Sprinkle by The Cat's Pajamas Rubber Stamps; You are the Hippest of Cats by Paper Candy

Dye Inkpads: Adirondack (Coffee) by Ranger Industries

Papers: White, Pink and Brown Cardstock: Local Craft Store; Ooh La La by Colorbok

Ribbons: Brown and Pink Striped and Polka Dot Ribbons: Local Craft Store

Adhesives: Double-Stick Tape; The Ultimate! Glue by Crafter's Pick; Glue Lines by Glue Dots International

Other: Rhinestones; Small Pink and Cream Buttons; Vintage Buckle

 tip! Think creatively when adding ribbon to your cards- thread through buckles, ribbon charms and eyelets. Fold or pink and attach bright ribbon snippets with colored staples.

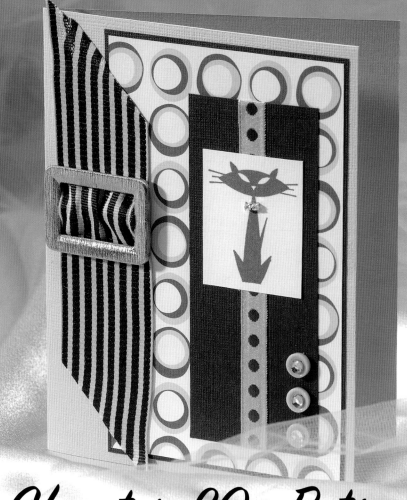

Chapter 20 · Pets

Anyone that has a pet, whether it's a frisky Golden Retriever puppy, a chatty parrot or a sophisticated Siamese cat, knows the joys of owning an animal! Pets can be our best friends. We cater to them, love them, care for them and miss them while we are away, as we do any beloved family member. Cards are a fun way of showing others that we understand the fondness they have for their precious pets.

instructions

1. Stamp Big Sprinkle on a piece of white cardstock using Coffee ink.
2. Secure a piece of pink polka dot ribbon and the stamped panel to a strip of brown cardstock using double-stick tape.
3. Layer the brown cardstock on patterned paper and another layer of brown cardstock, then mount on a folded pink card.
4. Thread a piece of wide ribbon through a vintage buckle, then secure to the card using Glue Lines.
5. Embellish the front of the card with tiny buttons and rhinestones.
6. Stamp Little Sprinkle and "You are the hippest of cats" on a piece of white cardstock using Coffee ink.
7. Layer over a piece of ribbon on the inside of the card using double-stick tape.

My Dog Likes You

Amy Wellenstein

materials

Rubber Stamps: Small Dog Bone by KK Originals; My Dog Likes You So You Must Be OK by Stampotique Originals; Dalmatian: Local Craft Store

Dye Inkpads: Archival (Carnation and True Blue) by Ranger Industries

Papers: White, Turquoise, Black and Pink Cardstock: Local Craft Store; Honeydew Melon from Lollipop Shoppe by Basic Grey

Ribbons: Pink Polka Dot Ribbon: Local Craft Store; Bubblegum Pink and Swimming Pool Rick Rack by Doodlebug Design: Local Craft Store

Tags: Local Office Supply

Buttons: Pink Buttons by Doodlebug Design

Adhesives: Foam Tape; Double-Stick Tape; The Ultimate! Glue by Crafter's Pick

Tools: Sewing Machine; Circle Punches by Marvy Uchida

instructions

1. Stamp Dalmatian on white cardstock using Carnation ink. Layer on black and turquoise cardstock panels.

2. Sew a piece of Swimming Pool rick rack to a panel of pink cardstock. Sew a piece of Bubblegum Pink rick rack to a patterned panel of cardstock.

3. Adhere both stitched panels to a folded turquoise card.

4. Use foam tape to attach the stamped panel to the card.

5. Use double-stick tape to attach a piece of pink polka dot ribbon across the top of the card.

6. Stamp Dog Bone on a small tag using Carnation ink. Adhere to card with foam tape.

7. Punch one large circle from patterned cardstock, one medium circle from aqua cardstock and one small circle from white cardstock.

8. Stamp phrase on the small circle.

9. Layer the circles and adhere to the inside of the card.

tip! Choose bright papers to make your card and stamp images in colored inks!

Lost at Sea

Amy Wellenstein

materials

Rubber Stamps: Mermaid Cat by Claudia Rose; Retro Wave by PrintWorks; I'm Lost at Sea Without You by Rubber Soul

Pigment Inkpads: VersaFine (Onyx Black) by Tsukineko

Dye Inkpads: Archival Ink (True Blue) by Ranger Industries

Papers: White Cardstock: Local Craft Store; Teal Wash by Christine Adolph for Creative Imaginations; Envy Mini Bangles by KI Memories; Sea Breeze Dotted Line by Doodlebug Design

Colored Pencils: Prismacolor (Lime Green and Brown) by Sanford

Metal Items: Swirly Ribbon Charm by Making Memories

Ribbons: Aqua Ribbon with Lime Green Edges by Offray: Local Craft Store

Buttons: Favorite Findings (Citrus) by Blumenthal Lansing Company

Adhesives: Foam Tape; Double-Stick Tape; Glue Stick; Mini Glue Dots by Glue Dots International; The Ultimate! Glue by Crafter's Pick

Other: Rhinestones; Chipboard

instructions

1. Adhere panels of teal wash and striped papers to a folded white card.

2. Adhere a panel of green patterned paper to a piece of chipboard (for stability).

3. Slide aqua ribbon through a ribbon charm and adhere it to the chipboard panel using double-stick tape (hiding the ends on the back side).

4. Mount the chipboard panel to the card using foam tape (for dimension).

5. Stamp Mermaid Cat on a piece of white cardstock using Onyx Black ink. Color with colored pencils.

6. Stamp Retro Wave below the cat image using True Blue ink.

7. Trim panel to size and adhere below the ribbon.

8. Further embellish the panel with buttons and small rhinestones.

9. For the inside of the card, stamp "I'm lost at sea without you" on a white panel using Onyx Black ink.

10. Stamp Retro Wave below the phrase using True Blue ink.

11. Mount stamped panel onto green patterned paper and adhere to the inside of the card.

Happy Birthday from the Cat

Amy Wellenstein

materials

Rubber Stamps: Birthday Cat with Balloons by PSX; Alphabet Set by Ephemera Design Studio

Dye Inkpads: Archival (Aqua and Carnation) by Ranger Industries

Hybrid Inkpads: Palette Hybrid (Chartreuse) by Stewart Superior

Papers: Green, Turquoise and White Cardstock: Local Craft Store; Bubblegum from Lollipop Shoppe by Basic Grey; Green Tea Bitty Blossom by KI Memories

Ribbons: Lime Green Satin Ribbon by Europa at Local Craft Store

Adhesives: Glue Stick; The Ultimate! Glue by Crafter's Pick; Double-Stick Tape

Other: Daisy (White); Rhinestone Brads; Pink Button

instructions

1. Cut and fold turquoise cardstock to make card.

2. Stamp Birthday Cat three times on white cardstock using carnation, chartreuse and aqua inks. Trim and layer onto turquoise and light green cardstocks.

3. Adhere layers to patterned paper, then to turquoise card.

5. Use double-stick tape to adhere a piece of lime green ribbon around the front of the card (place the seam on the front as seen in next step).

6. Cover the raw ends of the ribbon by gluing a white daisy at overlap of ribbon ends.

7. Embellish the daisy with a pink button and rhinestone brad.

8. For the inside of the card, stamp "HAPPY BIRTHDAY FROM THE CAT" on green floral paper using aqua ink and alphabet stamps.

9. Glue the patterned paper inside the card.

What in the World?

Amy Wellenstein

materials

Rubber Stamps: Suspicious Dog by Catslife Press; Asterisk Belt, Mod Car and Solid Quasar by The Cat's Pajamas Rubber Stamps; What in the World by River City Rubberworks

Pigment Inkpads: VersaFine (Onyx Black) by Tsukineko

Dye Inkpads: Archival (True Blue) by Ranger Industries; ColorBox Chalk (Lime Pastel) by Clearsnap

Papers: White, Brown and Aqua Cardstock: Local Craft Store; Pink Striped Paper: Local Craft Store; Pacific Delay (Turquoise and Green Stripe) by Scrapworks; Post-it Notes by 3M

Colored Pencils: Prismacolor (Brown and Yellow) by Stanford

Ribbons: Turquoise and Lime Green Reversible Ribbon with Stitched Edge by Textured Trios: Local Craft Store

Buttons: Favorite Findings Buttons (Citrus) by Blumenthal Lansing Company; Hand-Dyed Buttons (Bright Assortment) by Doodlebug Design

Adhesives: Foam Tape; Double-Stick Tape; The Ultimate! Glue by Crafter's Pick; Glue Stick

Other: Chipboard

instructions

1. Stamp Mod Car on white cardstock using Onyx Black ink.

2. Stamp the same image on a Post-it pad to create a mask. Trim the Post-it to create both positive and negative masks.

3. With the negative mask in place, stamp Suspicious Dog in the car.

4. Remove the negative mask and replace it with the positive mask.

5. Over-stamp the car with Asterisk Belt and Solid Quasar using Lime Pastel and True Blue inks respectively.

6. Remove mask and color dog with colored pencils.

7. Layer stamped panel on brown cardstock and pink striped paper.

8. Cut narrow slits above and below the stamped panel.

9. Reinforce a panel of green striped paper with chipboard.

10. Thread ribbons through the slits on the pink striped panel and secure to the green striped panel using double-stick tape (with ends hidden on the back side).

11. Create a folded card from reversible pink cardstock (solid on one side and striped on the other).

12. Mount the layered panel to the folded card and embellish with coordinating buttons.

13. Stamp Asterisk Belt on the inside of the card using True Blue ink.

14. Stamp "What in the World" on a scrap of white cardstock using Onyx Black ink. Layer on aqua cardstock and adhere to the inside of the card at an angle.

Just Chicken In On You

Amy Wellenstein

materials

Rubber Stamps: Striped Chicken by Claudia Rose; Lots of Circles by A Muse Artstamps; Alphabet Set by Brenda Walton for All Night Media/Plaid

Dye Inkpads: Archival Ink (True Blue) by Ranger Industries

Papers: Teal, Turquoise, White and Lime Green Cardstock: Local Craft Store; Striped Paper by MOD; Ice Cream Parlor (Simple Floral) by Pieces of Me by KI Memories

Ribbons: Lime Green and Aqua Sheer Ribbons by Midori: Local Craft Store

Buttons: Hand Dyed Buttons (Bright Assortment) by Doodlebug Design

Adhesives: Pop-Up Glue Dots by Glue Dots International; Foam Tape; Double-Stick Tape; Glue Stick

Other: Embroidery Floss (Turquoise)

Tools: Paper Cutter; Cosmetic Sponge

tip! Use clever puns for a smart card message.

instructions

1. Stamp chicken image on white cardstock using True Blue ink.

2. Layer on turquoise cardstock.

3. Stamp Lots of Circles on a panel of lime green cardstock using True Blue ink. Sponge ink around edges.

4. Adhere the panels together using foam tape.

5. Adhere loops of sheer ribbons to the back side of the panel using double-stick tape.

6. Layer on coordinating papers.

7. Stitch purple buttons in the corners using embroidery floss.

8. Mount the layered panel on a folded teal card.

9. Stamp "Just Chicken in on You" on white cardstock using True Blue ink.

10. Cut out the words, layer on coordinating panels of paper, and adhere to the inside of the card.

WOOF

Dawne Renee Pitts

materials

Rubber Stamps: Lissi's Frame and Best Friends by Stampotique Originals; Gothic Lowercase Alphabet by Postmodern Design; Dog by Judith; AB Seas Alphabet Set by Authentic Models

Dye Inkpads: Memories (Black) by Stewart Superior

Papers: Yellow Textured Cardstock by DieCuts with a View; Turquoise Cardstock: Local Craft Store

Metal Items: Yellow Dotlets by Doodlebug Design

Ribbons: Gingham Ribbon by Offray: Local Craft Store

Adhesives: Art Accentz Terrifically Tacky Tape by Provo Craft

Tools: Postage Stamp Scissors by Fiskars

tip! Nylon ribbon tends to fray. You can either go with the frays, as they add "character" or use pinking shears or very sharp scissors from Mundial to cut your ribbon.

instructions

1. Cut the yellow cardstock to make the pocket card.

2. Close the inside pocket with a strip of gingham ribbon and two Dotlets.

3. Punch holes along the bottom of card front.

4. Cut out strips of ribbons in varying lengths, and attach to the front of the card with the yellow Dotlets.

5. Cut a strip of turquoise cardstock to match the width of the cover and stamp with Lissi's Frame. Stamp "Woof" inside the frame.

6. Stamp Dog on the bottom right corner of the turquoise cardstock.

7. Attach the turquoise cardstock to the front of the card using the yellow Dotlets.

8. Stamp the Best Friends image on the turquoise cardstock and cut it out with the postage stamp scissors.

9. Stamp "FOR YOUR NEW" onto a piece of turquoise cardstock and cut out.

10. Attach the cardstock square and postage stamp to the inside of the card.

11. Put the gift card inside the card and give it to the new "parent" with love and pride.

Glamour Puss

Jill Haglund

materials

Rubber Stamps: Big Sprinkle (Cat Image) and Glamour Puss by The Cat's Pajamas Rubber Stamps; Label by Stampotique Originals

Dye Inkpads: Memories (Black) by Stewart Superior; Marvy Matchables (Bright Pink) by Marvy Uchida

Papers: White and Light Pink Cardstock: Local Craft Store; Pink Iron-On Fabric by K&Company; Pink Checked Paper, Pink Dotted Paper and Pink Striped Paper: Local Craft Store

Metal Items: Pink Brads by Making Memories

Fabric: White Tulle: Local Craft or Fabric Store

Ribbons: Black and White and Pink and White Gingham Ribbons: Local Craft Store

Adhesives: Glue Stick; Foam Tape; Glue Dots by Glue Dots International

Other: Pink Button

Tools: Paper Cutter; Two Sizes of Circle Punches by Marvy Uchida

instructions

1. Cut and fold white cardstock to make card.

2. Cut hot pink fabric to fit card and iron fabric onto card.

3. Cut and layer light pink cardstock and pink dotted paper as shown.

4. Cut a smaller piece of hot pink fabric and iron onto card.

5. Punch a large pink paper circle and a large pink fabric circle. Next, punch a smaller circle from the pink checked paper and stamp with Big Sprinkle image.

6. Adhere the large circles onto hot pink fabric square, with the fabric circle folded accordion-style and piece of tulle tucked behind the stamped checked circle. (Use foam tape to adhere due to bulk.)

7. Cut and fold small pink striped paper. Attach to bottom of the card as shown with glue stick; add brads to each side.

8. Stamp Label in black on white cardstock; stamp "Glamour Puss" in bright pink ink. Cut out label and glue to card front with glue stick.

9. Wrap ribbons around card and tie in tulle. Add button to top of bow with a Glue Dot.

tip! For the inside of the card, simply punch one or more large circles from pink and pink checked paper to write or stamp your message. Add another small image such as a stamped heart.

Let's Have A Party

Amy Wellenstein

materials

Rubber Stamps: Dog by Copper Leaf Designs; Large and Medium Alphabet Sets by Ephemera Design Studio; Party Hat by The Cat's Pajamas Rubber Stamps

Pigment Inkpads: VersaFine (Onyx Black) by Tsukineko

Papers: White, Aqua, Orange, Yellow and Pink Cardstock: Local Craft Store; Frenzy Ditty Dots by Paper Fever

Colored Pencils: Prismacolor Yellow, Aqua, Pink and Green by Stanford

Ribbons: Yellow Polka Dot Ribbon; Narrow Pink Ribbon, Aqua Ribbon with Green Dots and Orange Polka Dot Ribbon by Offray; Lime Green Satin Ribbon by Europa; Gingham Ribbon (Bubblegum & Limeade) by Doodlebug Design: Local Craft Store

Buttons: Colored Buttons by Doodlebug Design

Adhesives: Pop-Up Glue Dots by Glue Dots International; Double Stick Tape; The Ultimate! Glue by Crafter's Pick

Tools: Sewing Machine

tip! Your sewing machine can become your new favorite tool for making cards! All you need to know is a basic stitch to attach ribbons and rick rack.

instructions

1. Stamp Dog on white cardstock using Onyx Black ink. Color with colored pencils, then layer on pink and aqua cardstock panels.

2. Stamp Party Hat on a scrap of white cardstock. Color with colored pencils, cut out and adhere to the dog's head using foam tape.

3. Stitch coordinating ribbons onto a panel of patterned paper. Mount the panel on a folded orange card.

4. Use Pop-Up Glue Dots to adhere the stamped panel to the front of the card. Glue on coordinating buttons.

5. Stamp "Lets Have A Party" on yellow cardstock. Cut out the words, layer on coordinating papers and adhere to the inside of the card.

Chapter 21 · Let's Have a Party!

Some people will use any excuse for a party -- and why not?! Whether it's a luau, BBQ, birthday party or party just for party's sake, you'll need invitations. Here are some great ideas ... just add a small map and indicate the time, place and RSVP phone number. Don't yet know the details? Don't fret. These cards can be created now and specific info can be added later. Whatever the occasion, these colorful, whimsical cards will get anyone in the mood for Party Time!

Please Come To My Party

Amy Wellenstein

materials

Rubber Stamps: Alphabitties Alphabet Set by Stampotique Originals; Girls with Polka Dot Crowns by Tracy Roos for Peddlers Pack Stampworks

Dye Inkpads: Archival (Carnation) by Ranger Industries

Papers: White, Pink and Black Cardstock: Local Craft Store; Sparkle Dots by Pink from K.P. Kids & Co. by Paper Adventures

Tags: Clear Metal-Rimmed Tag: Local Craft Store

Ribbons: Polka Dot Ribbons (Pink and Orange) by Offray; Rick Rack (Bubblegum) by Doodlebug Design; Mini Rick Rack (Black); Gingham Ribbon (Tangerine/Bumblebee) by Doodlebug Design; Assorted Ribbons: Local Craft Store

Buttons: Hand-Dyed Buttons (Bright Assortment) by Doodlebug Design

Adhesives: Glue Stick; Double Stick Tape; Mini Glue Dots and Pop-Up Glue Dots by Glue Dots International; Foam Tape

Other: In Shapes Bloomers (Tropical) by Dress It Up Memory Mates by Jesse James & Co.

Tools: Paper Cutter; Sewing Machine

instructions

1. Stamp Girls on white cardstock using Carnation ink. Layer on black cardstock.

2. Stitch ribbon loops around the edge of a panel of black cardstock (the same size as the stamped panel).

3. Layer the panels on yellow polka dot paper, then mount on a folded pink card.

4. Embellish the stamped panel with colorful buttons and a clear metal-rimmed tag.

5. Use glue stick to adhere strips of the yellow polka dot paper to the inside of the card.

6. Stamp "Please Come to my Party" on white cardstock using Carnation ink.

7. Cut the words apart and layer on black cardstock; adhere to the inside of the card.

Summer Tea Party

Amy Wellenstein

materials

Rubber Stamps: Steam Swirl and Teacup with Spoon by The Cat's Pajamas Rubber Stamps; Lots of Flowers by A Muse Artstamps; Alphabet Set by River City Rubberworks

Dye Inkpads: Archival Ink (Carnation) and Adirondack (Lettuce) by Ranger Industries

Papers: White and Orange Cardstock: Local Craft Store; Perfect Pink Fine Weave (Homespun Collection) by Bo-Bunny Press; Petite Posies by Doodlebug Design; Simple Stripe (Summer) by KI Memories

Paints: Scrapbook Colors (Hibiscus) by Making Memories

Ribbons: Orange and Pink Plaid by May Arts: Local Craft Store

Adhesives: Foam Tape; Double-Stick Tape; The Ultimate! Glue by Crafter's Pick

Other: In Shapes Bloomers (Tropical) by Dress It Up Memory Mates by Jesse James & Co.; Gameboard Alphabet (Sadie – Spotlight) by Making Memories; Chipboard

instructions

1. Stamp Teacup and Steam Swirl on white cardstock using Lettuce ink. Layer on orange cardstock.

2. Stamp Lots of Flowers repeatedly on pink paper using Carnation ink.

3. Glue green flowers to the corners and set aside to dry.

4. Adhere panels of green floral and striped papers to a white cardstock base.

5. Wrap ribbon around the panel and secure the ends to the backside with double-stick tape.

6. Mount the panel to a folded white card.

7. Adhere the stamped panel to the card using foam tape.

8. Paint a chipboard "T" with pink paint and glue to the front of the card.

9. Adhere a strip of green floral paper inside the card.

10. Stamp "Please join me for a summer TEA" on orange cardstock using Carnation ink.

11. Cut out the words and adhere to the inside of the card.

Summer Party

Amy Wellenstein

materials

Rubber Stamps: Boo, Buga, and Uga (Tiki Mugs) by The Cat's Pajamas Rubber Stamps; Tall Alphabet by Stampotique Originals

Dye Inkpads: Archival (Aqua) by Ranger Industries; Adirondack (Oregano and "Name This Color" Blue) by Ranger Industries

Papers: White, Green, Khaki and Aqua Cardstock: Local Craft Store; Poolside Runway (Stripes) and Poolside Rhinestone (Dots) by KI Memories

Metal Items: 3/16" Silver Eyelets: Local Craft Store

Ribbons: Daiquiri by Making Memories: Local Craft Store

Buttons: Hand-Dyed Buttons (Bright Assortment) by Doodlebug Design

Adhesives: Foam Tape; Double-Stick Tape; The Ultimate! Glue by Crafter's Pick; Glue Stick

instructions

1. Stamp Uga, Buga and Boo (tiki mug stamp images) on white cardstock using Blue, Aqua and Oregano inks.

2. Layer on aqua and polka dot panels, then adhere to a wider strip of khaki cardstock.

3. Set silver eyelets on the ends of the strip and thread ribbon through. Secure ends on the back side using double-stick tape.

4. Adhere panel to a piece of striped paper using foam tape (for dimension), then mount on a folded green card.

5. Glue two aqua buttons to the ribbons.

6. Adhere a narrow strip of the polka dot paper across the inside of the card.

7. Stamp "PARTY" on a scrap of white cardstock using Aqua ink. Layer on green cardstock and adhere to the inside of the card.

BBQ Party Card
Amy Wellenstein

materials

Rubber Stamps: BBQ Grill by The Cat's Pajamas Rubber Stamps; Aloha Alphabet Set by Rusty Pickle

Pigment Inkpads: VersaFine (Satin Red) by Tsukineko

Papers: White, Red and Lime Green Cardstock: Local Craft Store; Red and White Gingham Check by Frances Meyer; Passion Word by Marah Johnson for Creative Imaginations

Metal Items: Flower Brads (Sherbet) by Making Memories

Ribbons: Lime Green Satin Ribbon by Europa; Gingham (Raspberry and Lime) by Doodlebug Design: Local Craft Store

Adhesives: Double-Stick Tape; Glue Stick; The Ultimate! Glue by Crafter's Pick

Other: Red Buttons

instructions

1. Stamp BBQ Grill twice on white cardstock using Satin Red ink.

2. Layer stamped panel on lime green cardstock and red patterned paper.

3. Wrap the layered panel with ribbon, securing ends on the back side with double-stick tape.

4. Glue red buttons along the bottom edge. Attach lime green flower brads down the right side.

5. Layer the panel on red checked paper and mount to a folded white card.

6. Stamp "BBQ PARTY" on lime green cardstock using Satin Red ink.

7. Layer on coordinating papers and adhere to the inside of the card.

It's a Stamp Party

Dawne Renee Pitts

> Gussie up,
> we're havin' a party

tip! Assorted ribbons and mixed alphabet stamps really jazz up a card!

materials

Rubber Stamps: Triangle Flag Strip by Postmodern Design; Dotted Line and Gussie Up by Stampotique Originals; Make Art by Catslife Press; Tall Alphabet by Stampotique Originals; Artistic Uppercase and Lowercase, Good Alphabet and Printers Type by Hero Arts; Mod Squares Perfectly Clear Stamps by Stampendous; Brenda Walton Alphabet by Plaid; Gothic Lowercase, Quirky Large and Front Page by Postmodern Design; Piccadilly Lower Case by PSX; Martin Brush Uppercase Alphabet by Creative Imaginations

Dye Inkpads: Memories (Black) by Stewart Superior

Hybrid Inkpads: Palette Hybrid (Lautrec Rainbow) by Stewart Superior

Papers: Blue, Lime Green, Orange, Bright Yellow and

Bright Pink Cardstock: Local Craft Store

Colored Pencils: Kimberly Watercolor Pencils by General Pencil Company

Metal Items: Colored Mini Brads by Making Memories

Ribbons: May Arts, Beaux Regards and Offray: Local Craft Store

Adhesives: Art Accentz Terrifically Tacky Tape by Provo Craft

Tools: Pinking Shears by Mundial

instructions

1. Cut and fold blue cardstock to make card.

2. Cut out a piece of lime green cardstock slightly smaller than card front.

3. Stamp the Stampotique Dotted Line on bright pink cardstock four times using black ink.

4. Use strips of the bright pink cardstock to make a frame around the outer edges of the lime green border, trim to fit.

5. Stamp Triangle Flag Strip two times on bright yellow cardstock. Use watercolor pencils to color in the flags.

6. Cut two pieces of the Triangle Flag Strip to fit inside the top and bottom of the pink frame.

7. Stamp Gussie Up on white cardstock. Cut out and pink one end. Attach to the lime green cardstock at a slight angle using the Making Memories colored mini brads.

8. Attach snips of various ribbons to the back of green cardstock around the two sides and top.

9. Attach the lime green cardstock panel to the card front.

10. Cut out a piece of lime green cardstock for the inside sentiment.

11. Stamp the information using a variety of rubber stamps; highlight certain letters with bright pink cardstock.

Product Resource Guide

3M / Scotch: www.scotchbrand.com

7gypsies: www.7gypsies.com

A Muse Artstamps: www.amuseartstamps.com

American Crafts: www.americancrafts.com

American Tag: www.americantag.net

Art Glitter: www.artglitter.com

Artic Frog: www.articfrog.com

Authentic Models: Local Craft Store

Awesome Albums: www.awesomealbums.com

Basic Grey: www.basicgrey.com

Bazzill Basics Paper: www.bazzillbasics.com

Beaux Regards: www.beauxregards.biz

Blumenthal Lansing Company: www.buttonsplus.com

Bo-Bunny Press: www.bobunny.com

Canson: www.canson.com

Catslife Press: www.catslifepress.com

Claudia Rose: www.claudiarose.com

Clearsnap, Inc.: www.clearsnap.com

Close to My Heart: www.closetomyheart.com

Colorbok: www.colorbok.com

Copper Leaf Design: Local Craft Store

Crafter's Pick: www.crafterspick.com

Creating Keepsakes: www.creatingkeepsakes.com

Creative Imaginations: www.cigift.com

DecoArt: www.decoart.com

Deluxe Designs: www.deluxecuts.com

DieCuts with a View: www.diecutswithaview.com

Doodlebug Design: 801-966-9952

Dress It Up: www.dressitup.com

Dymo: www.dymo.com

EK Success: www.eksuccess.com

Ephemera Design Studio: www.ephemeradesignstudio.com

Fibermark: www.fibermark.com

Fiskars: www.fiskars.com

FoofaLa: www.foofala.com; 1-800-588-6707

General Pencil Company: www.generalpencil.com

Glue Dots International LLC: www.gluedots.com

Grafix: www.grafixarts.com

Hampton Art: www.hamptonart.com

Heidi Swapp: www.heidiswapp.com

Hermafix: 1-888-CENTIS-6

Hero Arts: www.heroarts.com

Hot Potatoes: www.hotpotatoes.com

Impress Rubber Stamps: www.impressrubberstamps.com

Inkadinkado Rubber Stamps: www.inkadinkado.com

Just For Fun: www.jffstamps.com

K&Company: www.kandcompany.com

KI Memories: www.kimemories.com

KK Originals: www.kkoriginals.com

Li'l Davis Designs: www.lildavisdesigns.com

Magenta: www.magentarubberstamps.com

Making Memories: www.makingmemories.com

Marcella by Kay: Local Craft Store

Product Resource Guide Continued

Martha by Mail: www.marthabymail.com

Marvy Uchida: www.uchida.com

May Arts: www.mayarts.com

MOD Paper: www.loopcreations.com

me & my BIG ideas: www.meandmybigideas.com

Mundial: www.mundialusa.com

Offray: www.offray.com

Our Lady of Rubber: 520-432-2229

Paper Adventures: www.paperadventures.com

Paper Candy: www.papercandy.com

Paper Fever: www.paperfever.com

Paper Inspirations: www.paperinspirations.com

Paperfever: www.paperfever.com

Peddler's Pack Stampworks: www.peddlerspack.com

Plaid Enterprises, Inc.: www.plaidonline.com

Postmodern Design: 405-321-3176

PrintWorks Collection: www.printworkscollection.com

Provo Craft: www.provocraft.com

PSX: www.psxdesign.com

Ranger Industries, Inc.: www.rangerink.com

River City Rubberworks: www.rivercityrubberworks.com

Rubbermoon Stamp Company: www.rubbermoon.com

Rusty Pickle: www.rustypickle.com

Sakura of America: www.sakuraofamerica.com

Sandylion Sticker Designs: www.sandylion.com

Sanford: www.sanfordcorp.com

Savvy Stamps: www.savvystamps.com

Scenic Route Paper Company: www.scenicroutepaper.com

Scrapworks: www.scrapworks.com

SEI: www.shopsei.com

Sissix: www.sissix.com

Stampa Rosa: www.creativebeginnings.com

Stampcraft: www.eyreandbaxter.co.uk/

Stampendous: www.stampendous.com

Stampin' Up!: www.stampinup.com

Stampington & Company: www.stampington.com

Stampotique Originals: www.stampotique.com

Stamps by Judith: www.stampsbyjudith.com

Stewart Superior: www.stewartsuperior.com

Streamline Buttons: www.buttonsplus.com

Sue Dreamer: Local Craft Store

Suze Weinberg: www.schmoozewithsuze.com

The Cat's Pajamas Rubber Stamps: www.thecatspajamasrs.com

Therm O Web: www.thermoweb.com

Tsukineko: www.tsukineko.com

Turtle Press: www.turtlearts.com

Two Peas in a Bucket: www.twopeasinabucket.com

Uptown Design Company: www.uptowndesign.com

Whipper Snapper Designs: www.whippersnapperdesigns.com

Wordsworth: www.wordsworthstamps.com

Xyron: www.xyron.com